THE *Betty Crocker* HOME LIBRARY

GIFTS TO MAKE FOR LOVE OR MONEY

*A how-to book of imaginative ideas for
fun-giving or fund-raising*

by JANET and ALEX D'AMATO

GOLDEN PRESS • NEW YORK
Western Publishing Company, Inc.
Racine, Wisconsin

Photographs by Frank Stork

Library of Congress Catalog Card Number: 72-87344
GOLDEN and GOLDEN PRESS® are trademarks of Western Publishing Co., Inc.

Dear Friend,

What is the gift that best expresses your feelings about someone? The gift you make yourself. What is the gift that shows your personal devotion to a worthy cause? The gift you make yourself. And both prove the happy truth that giving indeed brings as much joy as getting.

There is another advantage as well. From the gift ideas in the chapters that follow, you can pick dozens that are artfully contrived from "recycled" throwaways. Yet their small cost hardly begins to indicate their value. This can only be measured in terms of the ingenuity, patience, and love that turn them from castoffs to keepsakes.

The good things to eat in Chapter 9 have been chosen to brighten almost any gift occasion and were tested in the Betty Crocker Kitchens. All other ideas have been carefully devised and developed by the authors, a talented husband-and-wife team—Janet D'Amato, writer, painter, and illustrator; and Alex D'Amato, book designer and commercial artist. Each is a creative craftsman.

Some projects in this book can be completed swiftly; others, demanding more time and skill, will reward you for painstaking effort. If you are looking for group projects, you will find many that are quick and easy to turn out on an assembly-line basis to stock a bazaar table.

Whatever you undertake—enjoy! Be venturesome—try your hand at something new. Surprise yourself with a talent you never knew you had. And, finally, be as pleased with your finished handiwork as someone will be to receive it.

Betty Crocker

Contents

COLOR ILLUSTRATIONS

Introduction

If you are fresh out of ideas for handmade gifts to surprise your favorite people, or to sell at a charity bazaar, this book will start your creative talents working again. It puts more than a hundred projects at your fingertips, with easy-to-follow instructions for completing them. So whether you prefer to dabble, stick, shape, bake, or sew, you will find something here that fits your ability and sparks your imagination.

This wide variety of projects has been planned for both beginning and seasoned crafters. Some of you may be interested primarily in new patterns and designs; others will want to follow step-by-step directions for mastering new techniques. Most of the projects end with a section headed "Variations" suggesting other ways to use the technique you have just learned. You'll soon have original ideas of your own.

As you work, you will discover an endless variety of useful materials. Many projects can be made with old or discarded items, or inexpensive trivia from variety or hardware stores. For instance, hardware items may be suddenly transformed into jewelry. Discards that might seem useless can be turned into attractive bazaar donations.

Throughout this book you will find new ways to use "throw-away" materials that will stimulate ideas for fresh, practical, inexpensive gifts. Start by keeping a "treasure box" handy for collecting such things as old or broken jewelry (beads, links, "jewels"), empty plastic bottles, blister wraps, notions, fabric scraps, hardware. The larger your selection, the easier it will be to find just the right shape, texture, or color for your project.

In general, when using discards, add something new, even if it's only a coat of paint. Affixing old, weary materials to discards never produces a happy result. But apply a fresh surface or sparkling trim to worn objects and you will be amazed to see how little ingenuity it takes to produce something vivid and exciting. Gifts should never look like disguised throwaways. Their humble source should remain a mystery.

If you need to work with new materials, buy wisely. Keep your eyes open as you shop. The very thing you need may appear in the most unlikely section of the store. If you stretch your imagination a bit, you will recognize it instantly. Search for interesting fabric remnants or upholstery shop samples that you can buy at modest prices. They won't look like bargains when converted into lovely gifts.

Sometimes you will find that basic materials come in larger quantities than you need for a single project, but you will undoubtedly use them again and again as your interest in crafts grows. Paint, brushes, varnish, glue are a few examples. If you divide the initial cost by the number of things you make, you will find that your original investment is a sound one, and that the cost of each project is really very small.

With the help of the instructions that follow, be resourceful and perfect your skills. Make something for yourself first. Then when you have gained a little experience and confidence, start making gifts for others or as donations for a bazaar. You will be surprised to discover how relaxing it is to keep your hands busy while the family watches TV. You will also enjoy the personal satisfaction to be gained from making something beautiful. You may even find your family begging to join in the fun and starting to work on projects of their own. There is something here for everyone.

1. BEFORE YOU START

MATERIALS

Local stores, as well as mail-order craft suppliers, are stocked with all sorts of useful materials, and new products are constantly appearing. Art supply, hardware, stationery, and variety shops also provide items needed to make the projects in this book. The most fertile sources, however, are the common discards that clutter most people's homes.

If you want to order materials by mail, request a catalog from Lee Wards, 1200 St. Charles Road, Elgin, Illinois 60120. There you will find beads, trims, paints, finishes, and many other useful supplies.

The following brief notes will help you to identify your needs and suggest sources for these materials.

ADHESIVE-BACKED VINYL

This is a great camouflager for old or discarded items. When the backing paper has been peeled off, it will stick to any smooth, clean surface. Many companies make this type of covering (CON-TACT ®, Adhere ® [Clopay Corporation], Cling ®, KWIK KOVER ®, etc,); each offers a special assortment of patterns, including many wood grains and interesting textures. These eliminate the need for glue, and the vinyl surface is both durable and easy to wash. You can also find adhesive-backed colored burlap, as well as foils and flocked textures.

CLAY

Craft-supply houses and art stores carry clay that shapes easily and dries hard in the air. Or you can prepare a simple homemade version (flour clay) to use for small objects. The recipe and instructions for flour clay are under Christmas Ornaments (see page 32).

CORK

Most craft stores and mail-order craft houses stock cork in sheets of various thicknesses. Some carry pre-cut squares and circles.

FABRICS

All fabrics for gift-making should be new, but scraps left from any sewing venture—slipcovers to dresses—can be used. If you need to buy fabric, check fabric department remnant counters. Sample squares can often be used for small items.

FELT

Felt is especially easy to use because the edges can't fray and it comes in a variety of colors. Purchase felt in ¼-yard pieces or in pre-cut squares.

FOAM RUBBER, ART FOAM

Foam rubber comes in sheets for upholstering, and it can usually be purchased by the foot in the thickness desired in drapery departments or upholstery shops.

Colorful sheets of "art foam," ⅛" thick, are available from craft suppliers and some variety and department stores.

FOIL

Aluminum-foil plates, cans, etc. are useful discards. Aluminum foil itself is also a handy craft material.

GESSO

This opaque undercoating can be applied like paint with a brush. (Wash brush with water.) It provides a firm coating over most surfaces, if you follow directions on the can. Gesso is available from craft and art-supply stores.

GLUES

The composition and effectiveness of glues are constantly being improved, making crafts much easier for the average person. There are many types of glues on the market today, so read their labels if you need one for a special purpose.

Epoxy glue, putty: Epoxy glues come in two separate tubes and must be mixed for use. Most of them are clear, and require very little to hold fast. There are many brands easily available, such as Devcon® Clear Epoxy. Some set in five minutes. Mix small amounts at a time, as directed. Epoxy makes a strong bond, but will adhere best on unpainted surfaces.

Most hardware stores carry epoxy putty, such as PC-7, in cans. An epoxy bond putty, made for fixing furniture, can be kneaded from slices of two sticks. It is clean and easy to handle. These putties hold together uneven surfaces, such as a curve against a flat surface, and make exceptionally strong bonds. Always follow manufacturer's instructions.

Household cement: Household cement, such as DUCO® Cement*, is a good adhesive for hard surfaces (such as glass or porcelain), metals, and certain small areas, since it is absolutely clear. Avoid its use on large areas, or on painted or vinyl surfaces; it can take the surface off.

Rubber cement: Another useful adhesive. Coat both surfaces with brush, usually provided in the container. When surfaces are dry, stick surfaces together, using your finger to rub off excess cement around the edges. This proves most practical with flimsy materials, as when affixing thin paper to lightweight cardboard. The paper will not wrinkle or curl as it does with glue.

White glues: When glue is mentioned throughout this book (without reference to a specific kind), a white glue (such as Elmer's Glue-All™ or AD-A-GRIP GLUE™) may be used. Most are available in plastic dispenser-type bottles. Good for large areas, they can be washed off when wet, and are best for most general jobs. White glues tend to thicken with time after opening, but you can thin them with water if necessary. They cannot be used on styrofoam.

TACKY® and SOBO™ are types of white glues that will be referred to in the instructions as "fabric glue," or "styrofoam glue," because of their success with those substances. The thicker one (TACKY) is good for edgings. These glues will not soak through fabrics, but check labels to determine most suitable uses and materials.

*Registered trademark of E.I. du Pont de Nemours & Co. (Inc.)

If you need a clamp to hold two surfaces together while glue dries, clip clothespins are ideal. Always keep some handy.

HARDWARE
The best source for bolts, nails, and other metal goods is, of course, the hardware store. Chains can be found in drapery departments, notion departments (chains used for weighting coats), and craft-supply stores. Chains can also be found among discards, old bracelets, belts, etc.

PAINTS
There are many kinds of paint available for finishing craft objects. If painting gifts for young children, use only those labeled "nontoxic."

Acrylic: Acrylic paints in tubes (Hyplar®, LIQUITEX® Acrylic Artists' Colors, and other brands) mix with water and dry waterproof. Since they dry very rapidly, wash brushes in water promptly after use.

Enamel: Enamel paints, sold in small cans, give a shiny, durable surface. After painting, your brush must be cleaned with turpentine, then washed with soap and water.

Fluorescent: Fluorescent paints, sold in sets of small jars, work well when extra-brilliant colors are needed. Basically these are water-color paints. Several coats may be needed to cover a surface adequately, and a clear finish coating (such as varnish) is recommended.

Latex: Household latex paints are similar to acrylic and come in many colors. Save leftovers from house painting chores. White latex serves as a good undercoating; it provides a good painting surface at the lowest cost. (For other undercoating, see Gesso.)

Poster paint: Inexpensive poster colors, in jars, are not waterproof or durable but can be substituted for more durable paints. If you use them on a craft project, it is necessary to add a permanent finish. When the painted surface has dried, spray on varnish, then brush on several coats of varnish (or add a plastic coating or shellac over the paint).

Rub-on metallic: Rub-on finishes in tubes or jars (RUB'N BUFF®, TREASURE GOLD™, etc.) are most useful for covering small raised areas and for giving a metallic glow along the edge or tip of an object.

Spray paint: Although spray paints are somewhat more expensive than paint in the can, they are easy to handle and convenient, especially for small items. There are many colors available, even fluorescent ones. Buy these as needed for a specific project.

PAPER

Plain paper is needed for enlarging patterns or for planning or drawing designs. Lightweight paper can be used for tracing and completing half-patterns and tracing actual-size patterns right from the book. Thin typing paper will do, but art stores carry pads of tracing paper which is even better for this purpose.

PAPIER-MÂCHÉ

Papier-mâché can be shaped into delightful objects. There are excellent prepared mixes on the market (such as CELLUCLAY ®) which will be referred to as "prepared papier-mâché." Add water as directed on the package, and you are ready to work. (See page 13.)

Papier-mâché can be made at home by soaking small squares of newspaper in water. When mushy, squeeze out the water and add wallpaper paste until the consistency is puttylike but not sticky. Making papier-mâché seems a rather long procedure, and the results of the homemade product are sometimes uneven.

STYROFOAM

Most craft and some variety stores carry styrofoam. Around the Christmas holidays one finds it everywhere, either in sheets or in various shapes, such as balls and cones. Purchased items often come packed in styrofoam that can be reused in craft projects. Easily cut with a coping saw or serrated kitchen knife, styrofoam must be assembled with glue especially made for it. (Check the label on the glue container.)

TAPES:

Fabric and plastic tape: There are colored tapes of various widths of either fabric or plastic which make sturdy joinings or can be used for decorations.

Masking tape: Masking tape is useful for holding patterns in place, or holding small pieces together while glue sets. Double-stick masking tape has adhesive on both sides.

Transparent tape: Transparent tape is needed for wrapping gifts and a variety of other uses. Keep a roll handy. Useful also: double-stick transparent tape.

TRIMS

Trims of all sorts give gifts a boutique elegance. Fabric and variety stores and craft-supply shops have a selection.

Beads, sequins, jewels: Beads, fake jewels, paillettes, sequins, and other sparkling trims can make lavish gifts out of ordinary items. Pieces of old jewelry (pearls, beads, chains, glass jewels, etc.) can provide many treasures. Some variety and fabric stores carry seed beads, rhinestones, and flat-backed jewels to sew or glue in place. Most craft-supply shops have a large assortment of beads and jewels, including plastic beads by the yard, that can be glued around an object like an edging. Plastic beads are also sold as jewelry. (One necklace goes a long way when used in crafts.)

Edgings: There are woven fabric trims, braids, laces, and edgings (such as soutache, rickrack, middy braid, etc.) in a wide range of colors. Embroidered edgings come in a variety of colors and patterns. Craft-supply houses and some fabric and variety stores carry several kinds of gold and silver trims. Some now come with adhesive backing. Most fabric trims are made to be sewn or glued in place. (See page 3 for gluing tips.)

Metallic and other cords: Card and gift shops carry gift-tie cords in gold, silver, and other metallic colors. These are inexpensive and very elegant. Metallic cords are also available by the yard from craft stores. Lace, velvet, and yarn gift ties can also be used.

Paper foil: Craft stores carry paper-foil edgings, round motifs of embossed gold foil. Foil motifs are often available in variety stores around Christmas for gift trims. Stationery stores carry stars, sometimes snowflakes, and other motifs.

Yarn: Yarn can often be used as a trim. You'll probably use pieces left over from knitting projects. For crafts, the fiber content does not usually matter. You can use whatever is available. Select yarn for color and size. Jumbo yarns are especially effective.

VARNISH AND FINISHES

A can of spray varnish is very useful to keep around at all times. For a heavier protective coating, buy a can of regular varnish and keep a special brush just for varnishing. Varnish can be purchased in either matte or gloss finish.

Plastic coatings: Other clear protective coatings are made of various plastics (such as Hyplar™ Medium Varnish). New ones become available constantly. Ask about them at your hardware, craft, or art store.

Shellac: Can be used instead of varnish or plastic coatings in most cases. Because it has an alcohol base, it dries rapidly. Use a fresh supply; old shellac may become tacky. Follow instructions on can. It is not recommended for any project to be used outdoors.

VELCRO®

Available in notions and fabric stores, VELCRO® Brand Fastener comes in two strips of interlocking textures. Cut it to the length needed and sew one strip on each side of an opening. To close, press together; to open, pull apart.

WOOD

If possible, use real wood; it lends a special quality to gifts. Lumber yards often have scraps. Anyone with a workshop usually has small leftover pieces of lumber. For a small fee, lumber dealers will usually cut purchased lumber to the size you want.

Shapes: The toy departments of some variety stores carry bags of wood turnings that contain useful pieces. Lumber yards have an assortment of precut decorative wood units, finials, and turnings available, but these are sometimes expensive.

Boxes: Unfinished boxes are available from craft stores or from mail-order craft-supply companies. Often old boxes can be sanded and refinished.

Used wood: Some sources of second-hand wood are described under driftwood bases (see page 19). All wood should be sanded smooth before finishing.

TOOLS

All crafts in this book are designed to be made with hand tools, such as hand drill, coping saw, pliers, and screwdriver. A basement workshop would be handy but not necessary.

Awl: Another necessary tool to have around is an awl for making holes. It is available in variety and hardware stores.

Knives and razor blades: Single-edged razor blades are necessary for some projects — handle them carefully. Craft and art stores carry handles to hold razor blades, which are easier on fingers when a lot of cutting is involved. A utility knife (X-acto®, available in art stores) has a pencil-shaped handle and holds a slanted razor-sharp blade. It is most efficient for inside cuts and precise cutting. A mat knife is good for cutting cardboard and other heavier materials.

Scissors: Keep them handy at all times. They will not be listed under "Materials" in the instructions, since they are necessary for almost every project. Keep a good pair for fabrics and trims to get a good clean cut. Use an old pair for paper, foil, etc. Manicure scissors are helpful in some projects where cutting small curved areas is required.

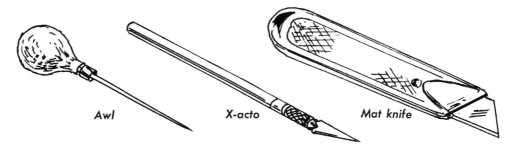

Awl   X-acto   Mat knife

WORK AREAS

When using glue, paint, or any materials of this nature, be sure to protect work surfaces and clothing. Wear an apron or smock and spread newspapers over table tops. Use rubber or plastic gloves to protect your hands when dyeing or painting.

Follow directions on all cans, bottles, packages, etc. Take any precautions the manufacturer suggests. When spray-painting, protect all surrounding surfaces. Place the object in a corrugated box either outdoors or in a well ventilated room.

PATTERNS

When necessary, a small-scale pattern is provided for enlargement. Here is a simple way to do it.

On a piece of paper, draw the same number of squares as appear on the pattern. Make them the size indicated (e.g., each square equals ½″). The large squares will correspond to the small squares on the pattern (Fig. 1). Start drawing where a pattern line touches an edge. Count the squares and draw the outline of the pattern as it is positioned on the corresponding (smaller) squares. This will give you the enlarged pattern (Fig. 2).

(Each square = ½″.)

1

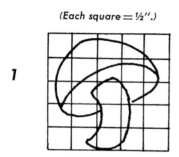

Pattern as it appears in the book

2

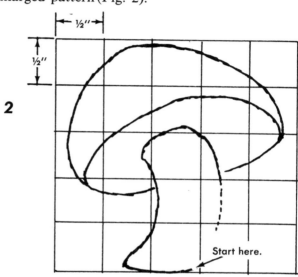

Start here.

Your drawing for pattern to be used

Sometimes a half-pattern is indicated by a broken (fold) line (Fig. 3). After enlarging it, trace this half on lightweight paper. Fold paper along broken line and trace other half from your first tracing. Open paper and pattern is complete.

If your fabric is lightweight, you can place the enlarged half-pattern on a fold of the material and cut both halves at once (Fig. 4).

3

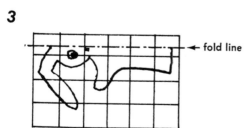

← fold line

4

fold line →

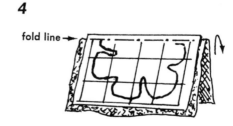

2. DECORATIVE GIFTS FOR THE HOME

Inspired ideas for home decorating may come from many sources, but the most interesting furnishing schemes tend to emphasize a room's focal point. Individual use of crafts can often liven such a room, giving it style, accent, and character.

Today many people are inventing their own accessories, to make décors more exciting. In this chapter, various craft techniques will be discussed, with directions for specific projects. Selecting one of these as your own, you can brighten a drab corner while gaining assurance as a decorator. Any of these finished projects becomes giftworthy if the maker simply notes the general theme and dominant colors of the recipient's home. It should be easy to adjust textures and colors as the project progresses, and this results in a more personal gift.

There are many occasions for such presents: housewarmings, holiday visits, weddings, anniversaries, for examples. A unique, well-made, hand-crafted gift is always welcome.

COASTERS

When jar tops accumulate, resist the temptation to throw them away. With a little effort and imagination, you can transform them into coasters. Any top, plastic or metal, about 3″ across, is usable.

See color photograph facing page 41.

MATERIALS NEEDED

4 matching jar tops (about 3″ in diameter, 1″ high)
1½ yds. small drapery weights
1½ yds. white decorative fabric edging or trims (about ½″ wide)
1½ yds. cord or twine
6″ × 6″ piece of sheet cork (or sheet of art foam that size)
6½″ × 6½″ piece of felt (plain or stick-on type)
Gloss white spray paint
Gold rub-on metallic finish
White glue
Also needed: Clip clothespin, single-edged razor blade with holder, old clean brush

1

CUT CIRCLES: Remove cardboard liner from inside top. Use as a pattern for cork or art foam liner. Cut circle out of cork (or art foam). On felt, trace around outside of jar top and then cut felt circle for base. Cut enough for four tops. Set circles aside.

2

Cut here.

DECORATE BASE EDGE: Use drapery weights as the base row of decoration on the coaster, to give stability to plastic tops. The weights are small pellets enclosed in a fabric tube. You can buy them by the yard. With white glue, attach strip of drapery weights around base edge of cover (Fig. 1). To make a neat joining where ends meet, allow a slight overlap and leave about ½″ on each side of it unglued. When glued portion is dry, cut overlap with a razor blade (Fig. 2) or knife, so ends butt against each other. Glue down.

3

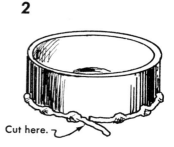

When base edging is dry, glue on a row of decorative fabric trim (or paper trim, if preferred) around middle. Hold with clip clothespin until dry (Fig. 3). Butt ends as described above. Edge with glued cord, using same procedure. Repeat, decorating other three tops.

TO FINISH: When all trims are in position and dry, add a finishing coat. Dilute white glue: 2 parts glue to 1 part water. With a brush, apply coating to outside of coaster. Let it soak into the fabric trims but brush

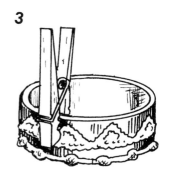

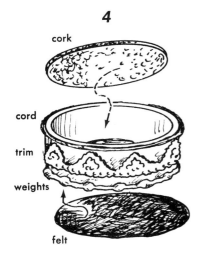

4

cork

cord

trim

weights

felt

out any excess so there are no blobs. Wash brush immediately. When glue is dry, apply a second coat.

Allow to dry very thoroughly. Spray coaster with white paint inside and out. It may take several coats to achieve a rich gloss white. Be sure to allow each coat to dry before adding another. When paint is dry, add gold. Using ball of finger, rub on metallic finish sensitively. Feel the texture, so the metallic color highlights only the raised areas, leaving the background untouched.

TO ASSEMBLE: Add a dab of glue in center and insert cork (or foam) circle inside each coaster (Fig. 4). Glue felt circle to bottom of coasters to protect table tops.

VARIATIONS

For shallower tops (3½″ in diameter, ½″ high, such as metal fruit-jar tops), use narrower trim (Fig. 5). Metal tops are heavy enough; you won't need to add the weights. Improvise your trimming according to the width you need to decorate.

Other effective color combinations can be used: spray black, rub-on silver; spray brown, rub-on gold or copper; spray red, rub-on gold.

5

POTTERY-LIKE VASES

See color photograph facing page 41.

You don't have to be an experienced potter to transform an ordinary bottle into a vase that looks like painted pottery. Instead of working with clay on a potter's wheel, you use papier-mâché and a small turntable or lazy Susan. Papier-mâché can be dented, smoothed, or shaped in much the same way as clay, but it requires no firing to give it a hard finish. You can make a vase like the Indian-inspired one shown, or choose any bottle available; then decide on the general shape and decorations you would like to make.

MATERIALS NEEDED

Throwaway glass bottle (neck should be large enough to use as vase)
Prepared papier-mâché
Newspaper
Wallpaper paste (available wherever wallpaper is sold)
Paint (preferably acrylic)
Gesso (or white latex paint)
Varnish (and brush cleaner), or clear plastic finish
Also needed: Turntable (such as used for spices), fine sandpaper,
   large brush ½″ to 1″ (for gesso, varnish and paint), small round
   brush (for painting designs), knife, old bowl about 1 qt. size (to
   mix paste, clean, use for mixing mâché), small old dish

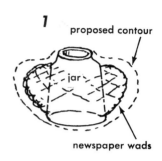

1

proposed contour

jar

newspaper wads

CHOOSE a bottle to use as a base. For the wide Indian vase shown,
a large-size instant-coffee jar was used as a core. Fruit-juice containers
would be good for taller vases.

2

wads

strips

TO SHAPE NEW CONTOURS: The bulk of the new contour is
created by adding newspaper wads (Fig. 1). Tear newspaper in strips
about 1″ × 4″. For bigger wads use larger strips. Mix about a cupful of
wallpaper paste with water until it is the consistency of thin pudding. Soak
the newspaper strips in wallpaper paste. Dip wads in paste and lay around
bottle. Pull strips out of the paste, removing excess paste with fingers. Use
strips like sticky tape to hold wads in position desired. Lay pieces over and
around wads and smooth down onto bottle (Fig. 2). Build up shape with
more strips until wads are covered and you are satisfied that there is
sufficient bulge to bottle where you want it (Fig. 3). Remember, there will
be at least another ¼″ layer over this. Be sure to allow newspaper to dry
thoroughly before starting next step.

3

MIX PREPARED PAPIER-MÂCHÉ according to directions. Lay globs of
it around the bottle and newspaper, and press firmly against them with
palms of the hands.

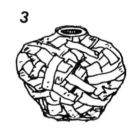

4

papier-mâché

¼″ lip

Place bottle on turntable; keep turning and shaping. Make papier-
mâché thicker where necessary. The old bottle should be well disguised
by now. Covering should be at least ¼″ thick at the thinnest spot
(Fig. 4). As you turn, check the outside contour. You'll notice some places
need more thickness, some less, to make the vase more symmetrical; but
some irregularities in shape will give it a "handmade artifact" look. Keep

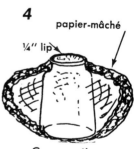

Cross section

a dish of water handy and keep hands moist as you work. The mâché can be pulled off, pushed over, or shaped any way you like. With a knife, flatten top to make an even layer about ¼″ above glass.

When you are satisfied with the shape, smooth over the entire surface with wet hands. *Allow to dry thoroughly.* It may take a week or more, but less time in hot, dry climates. When dry, sand the surface lightly.

PAINT   the surface with gesso for a base coating. Allow to dry. Then sand and give a second coat, for a smoother finish. When the second coat of gesso is dry, paint vase in color desired. To make the illustrated vase, paint first coat in medium tan. After the paint has dried, gently brush over a second coat of a much lighter tan, hitting the high spots only. This achieves a pottery-like texture.

When paint is dry, sketch in the design with a pencil. All early cultures used similar motifs; the line, circle, zigzag, and spiral. These are easy to do and can be combined into beautiful designs. Repeat units, using motifs suggested (Fig. 5), or create your own. Make units wider or narrower as necessary to fit around shape. On the Indian vase, use terra-cotta red and black for the design. If paint is too thick for use in details of design, thin with water to a good workable consistency. Paint designs on the vase.

When paint is dry, cover with a finishing coat (varnish or plastic). When this has dried, turn over and finish bottom.

Motif to paint on
upper portion of vase

top of jar

5

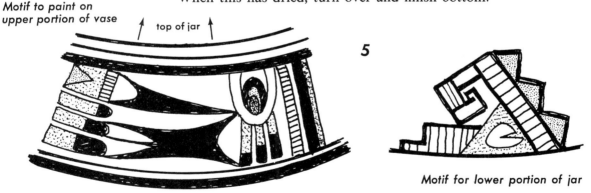

Motif for lower portion of jar

VARIATIONS

The variety of shapes you can make with papier-mâché is endless. If you run out of ideas, the ancient artifacts in museums or art books will give you the inspiration you need. If you do not care to paint designs, cut motifs from decorative paper and glue on vase. Finish as before.

Texturing can be added by pressing shapes into the wet papier-mâché as you work. Press in a knife tip, button, potato masher, etc. Experiment with various effects. You can always wet your fingers, rub out the design, and try again. To make an indentation that circles the vase, hold the tip of a knife against the vase as you rotate the turntable (Fig. 6).

Not only vases but all sorts of figurines, animals, decorative dishes, etc., can be made with this method. The core doesn't necessarily have to be a bottle. It can be wire, wood, cardboard — anything that will serve as a base on which to form the shape you want.

HARDWARE TRIVET

The trivet shown is made of metal nuts to be found in any hardware store. Or you might beg some from a friend whose collection is gathering rust in his toolbox. If there is a factory near you, try to pick up their small metal rejects. You may find more interesting shapes in a plant than anywhere else, and the cost (if any) is negligible.

MATERIALS NEEDED
Lid from a metal container (type used for cookies, candies, nuts, etc.,
    minimum diameter 6″)
Hardware items: twenty ¾″ nuts (outside diameter); three 1¼″
    (outside diameter) flat washers; six ⅜″ nuts; four ½″ nuts
Cardboard (optional)
Black spray paint
Silver spray paint
Spray varnish (optional)
Four ½″ square scraps of black felt
20″ silver cord (gift wrap or soutache)
White glue (for cardboard)
Household cement (for metals)
Also needed: Rust remover (optional)

PREPARE LID: Spray lid black inside and out.

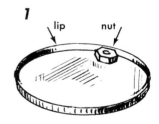

ADJUST HEIGHT OF NUTS: Place one ¾″ nut inside the lid when paint is dry. Check to see if it is the proper height (Fig. 1). If nut is a little higher than lip of lid, that's fine. If it is below edge, cut a circle of cardboard the size of the top and glue it down inside. If top of nut is still below edge of lid, add another circle of cardboard. Paint cardboard black. Make sure the nuts, or other items to be used, are all uniform in height.

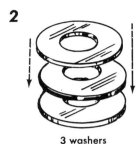

2

3 washers

3

center decoration

3 washers {

To plan center decoration, pile up the three washers (Fig. 2), place the six small nuts (⅜″ diameter) around the top of washers (Fig. 3). Adjust if necessary. Top surface of all nuts must be level. Remove the hardware.

PREPARE HARDWARE: If you are using old nuts or other rusty hardware, soak the pieces in rust remover. (Follow instructions on container.) Clean and dry all units. Then spray silver. New hardware is usually a natural shiny silver which will need no cleaning or painting.

ARRANGE AND GLUE: Place the units in the cover to make an attractive arrangement. When you are satisfied with the design, glue nuts in place with household cement. Glue down a few at a time and let them set. Then you won't disturb them when you pick up others to be glued. Glue in center decoration, gluing all parts to each other first, then onto lid.

TO FINISH: When all pieces in the lid are set and glue is dry, turn over, and with household cement, glue on the four ½″ nuts at even intervals around the base for "feet."

Using white glue, add a piece of felt to bottom of each nut used for "feet." When glue is dry, trim off felt to edge of nut with small scissors.

Measure the circumference of the lid, cut a piece of silver cord to fit, and glue it around outside of rim. Apply spray varnish lightly over entire unit for added durability.

CANDLESTICKS

Although the candlestick pictured here may look as though it is formed of one piece of wood — carved or turned on a lathe to create an interesting shape — it is actually a composite of several small units. Spools, knobs, drapery rings, and finials are used to achieve this effect.

MATERIALS NEEDED
Selection of wooden knobs, spools, a drapery finial, wooden drapery
     rings, etc. (see Fig. 1)
Candle socket (from a craft shop), or a 1″ nail
3″ gold cord (optional)
Stain or paint, varnish
White glue

See color photograph facing page 41.

Also needed: Saw, brush for stain, brush for varnish, brush for paint, damp rag

PLAN CANDLESTICK: To make the candlestick pictured here, various wooden pieces are stacked and glued together. Fig. 1 shows specific shapes and sizes, but you can choose your own. To design a candlestick of good proportion, place larger sections at the bottom. Select units of different heights; variety makes the candlestick more unusual and attractive.

PREPARE UNITS: Saw tip off drapery finial. Smooth and sand all pieces.

The top piece is a flat wooden disk ⅛″ thick. This can be made by sawing off a piece of spool or knob rim. Most craft shops carry metal candle sockets with screws attached for fastening into wood. Some even have a drip dish, which eliminates the need for top disk (Fig. 2).

If you can't buy these sockets, make a spike to accommodate candles of various sizes. Hammer a 1″ nail up through center of top flat disk (Fig. 3).

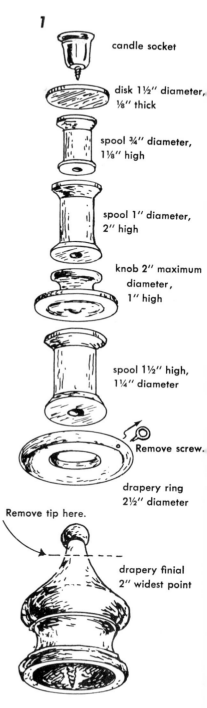

1

candle socket

disk 1½″ diameter, ⅛″ thick

spool ¾″ diameter, 1⅛″ high

spool 1″ diameter, 2″ high

knob 2″ maximum diameter, 1″ high

spool 1½″ high, 1¼″ diameter

Remove screw.

drapery ring 2½″ diameter

Remove tip here.

drapery finial 2″ widest point

knob 2¾″ maximum diameter

2

candle socket with drip dish

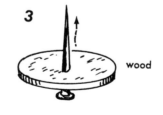

3

wood

TO ASSEMBLE: Stack wooden parts together to be sure they fit and make a pleasing arrangement. With white glue, attach pieces to each other. Glue together two at a time. If you attempt to glue the whole pile at once, you will have difficulty keeping it straight. As soon as two units are dry and firm, add the next. With a wet rag, remove any glue that oozes out; stain will not cover these spots.

TO FINISH: When all glue is dry and secure, give wood a coat of brown wood stain. Allow to set, according to instructions on can. Wipe off to reveal the grain. When dry, apply several coats of matte finish varnish.

If you prefer, you can finish the candlestick with household paint. Choose a rich color to complement the room. To achieve an antique look,

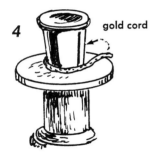

4   gold cord

apply a coat of stain when paint is dry. Using a clean rag, wipe it off immediately.

If you use a metal candle socket, glue a piece of gold cord around base of socket (Fig. 4) as a decorative finishing touch.

VARIATIONS
Discarded furniture legs (turnings) can often be cut to an appropriate size for a candlestick. Glue on wooden pieces for base and top before finishing.

NATURE'S SCULPTURES

Some of the most arresting sculptures are fashioned by nature: driftwood in its myriad shapes, curious shells, alluring rocks. These unspoiled treasures have such intrinsic charm that trying to improve them often mars their native beauty. Some processing may be needed to transform them into accessories, but do not hide or distort their natural features. Whenever possible, retain their subtle, original hues, which are often lovelier than any color you can add. And remember that a spontaneous form can be spoiled by lavish trims or clever touches. Here is a suggestion for mounting a piece of driftwood.

MATERIALS NEEDED
Piece of driftwood 5″ to 20″ high
Wooden base
Black paint
Green felt (size of base)
White glue (for wood)
Fabric glue (for felt)
Shell (or other natural accessories)
1½″ to 2″ nail or screw (for a larger piece)
Also needed: Saw, stiff brush, sandpaper

STUDY YOUR PIECE of driftwood carefully. Set it on the table in different positions until one angle seems to be the most exciting and attractive (like a piece of contemporary sculpture). When it is held at this angle, a certain part will probably have to be removed to make a flat surface to attach to the base. Mark the angle and saw off excess (Fig. 1).

CLEAN and wash the piece thoroughly with a stiff brush. Since most driftwood is beautifully toned in its natural state, it rarely needs varnish or coating of any sort. There are special driftwood finishes available from craft shops if you should want them.

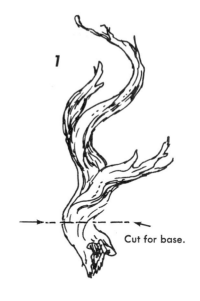

1

Cut for base.

BASE: Select a piece of wood suitable in size for the driftwood. Try to achieve a pleasing proportion between base and driftwood. Use ½″ or ¾″ lumber, cut to size needed. Sand smooth. Paint base black or finish in natural wood color.

TO MOUNT DRIFTWOOD: If the piece is small, just glue it to the base. For larger pieces, insert nail or screw up through base from the bottom (Fig. 2). Screw and glue onto bottom of the driftwood. If it doesn't balance—some tend to be tippy—you may have to remove a piece and cut it at a different angle to prevent its leaning too far in any direction.

TO COMPLETE: After attaching the piece to the base, add a small natural accessory or two. Tuck a dried flower in the curve of the drift-wood, or glue a shell or piece of coral to the base to give the illusion of something just washed up from the sea. Geological specimens and crystals are both attractive and appropriate. The combination you select will reflect your appreciation of nature and your own good taste.

Glue green felt to base so the piece can safely grace your finest furniture.

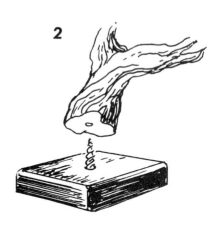

2

VARIATIONS
Suggestions for other bases for driftwood (Fig. 3): chopping block, cutting board, individual round wooden salad bowl (inverted), half a hamburger press, wooden coaster (inverted, for tiny pieces). Some craft shops and garden-supply stores carry bases of flat, irregularly shaped wood for this purpose.

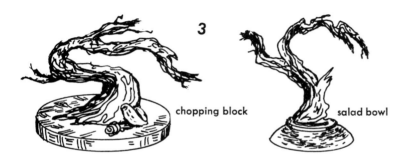

3

chopping block   salad bowl

coaster

Various suggestions for bases

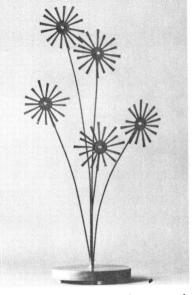

See color photograph facing page 57.

METAL FLOWER ARRANGEMENT

Here is a stylized fake-flower decoration to add a modern touch to any home. An inexpensive wood base might be practical if cost is a consideration, but for a gift, the lovely quality of a chopping board will add elegance to the piece.

MATERIALS NEEDED

Five 1¼″, five 1″, five ¾″ flat metal washers (diameters measured to outside edges)

Forty 2½″ and forty 2″ floor nails (the kind that are square at the tips)

5 wire hangers

1 round wooden chopping board, approximately 8″ diameter, or piece of wood 8″ square and at least 1″ thick

5 large pearls or jewels (from old jewelry) or small round filigree ornaments (sold with jewelry findings).

Epoxy putty

Household cement

Flat black spray paint

Rub-on type gold finish

Also needed: Metal file, cutting pliers or shears, knife, ⅜″ hand drill

STEMS: Cut the five wire hangers as shown (Fig. 1). Straighten out. Cut into the following lengths: 13½″, 17″, 18½″, 23″, 26″.

TO PREPARE METAL: Remove coating from the tips of all the nails with a metal file so that epoxy putty will adhere properly. Mix the epoxy putty according to directions. The putty sets better if you work in a warm room.

TO ASSEMBLE FLOWERS: Lay 1¼″ diameter washer flat and put layer of putty on it. Arrange eight 2½″ nails, spacing them symmetrically (Fig. 2). Between these, place eight 2″ nails. Adjust spacing. Lay tip of one stem (straightened coat hanger) across the washer (Fig. 3) and adjust nails around it. Add more putty over nails. Place 1″ washer over all units, sandwiching nails and stem between washers.

Press down so that putty remains firm against all units. Remove any

1

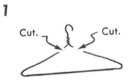

Cut. ← → Cut.

2

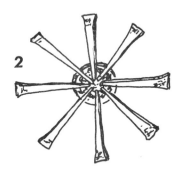

3

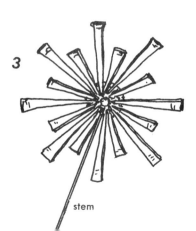

stem

excess putty with the tip of a knife, wiping off knife while putty is still soft. Apply a little putty to the ¾″ washer, and stick this in the center of the larger washer (on front).

Repeat process to make five flowers. Allow to set at least 24 hours (time varies with epoxy brands). Putty will become very hard.

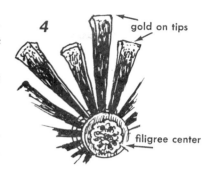

TO FINISH: Spray units with black paint. Allow to dry. With a gold rub-on type finish (or silver, if you prefer), rub the tip of each nail. Blend rub-on finish lightly toward the center, but leave most of the nail black (Fig. 4).

With household cement, glue decorative element (pearl, gold bead or filigree piece) into center hole.

TO MAKE BASE: Drill a ⅜″ hole in the center of a chopping board. Insert ends of stems. Arrange and bend stems slightly to achieve the effect shown in the photograph. Mix a little putty for hole in base, to hold the stems securely. (Wipe off excess while putty is still soft.)

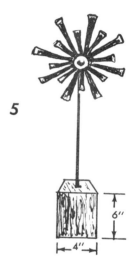

VARIATIONS

If you wish to start with something smaller, make one flower on a 12″ stem. For base, use a piece of 4″ × 4″ wood about 6″ high or 4″ cube. Lumber yards may have scraps or will cut it for you. (See page 19 for other wood bases.) Paint the wood black. Drill a small hole and insert the flower stem (Fig. 5).

OWL COLLAGE

This unusual owl, made of common household objects, can be a great conversation piece as well as a fanciful addition to a home. It is a dimensional collage, big enough to be noticed and to stir interest when shown in a room or at any bazaar.

MATERIALS NEEDED
12″ × 23½″ sheet of styrofoam, 1″ thick
12″ × 23½″ adhesive-backed blue burlap
½ yd. black cord or soutache braid
1 yd. black middy braid
3 black map tacks, box of white map tacks

See color photograph facing page 57.

7 white thumbtacks, 8 gold upholstery tacks
Box of blued sheet-rock nails
Box of yellow and white golf tees (approximately 100 units)
Box of yellow birthday-candle holders and enough white beads for
    centers
2 black beads, ¼″ diameter
Disposable plastic dispenser (from transparent tape)
2 yardsticks
Black paint (spray or brush)
Gold and white spray paint
Eight ½″ finishing nails
Screw-on type hanger
Styrofoam glue
Also needed: Coping saw or serrated knife, tweezers

BACKGROUND: Use styrofoam sheet, full width. Cut to 23½″ long with a serrated knife or coping saw. Cut piece of burlap the same size. Peel off backing and stick onto surface of the styrofoam.

FRAME: Saw two yardsticks 24″ long for side pieces. Remaining pieces of yardsticks should fit top and bottom of panel to complete frame. Check and adjust size (width of styrofoam may vary). Sand off yardstick printing, and paint black. Set aside.

ENLARGE PATTERN of owl picture on paper. If you want to save it (the original will be torn up as it is used), trace another pattern onto tissue paper.
    Mark height of the branch from pattern. Glue braids across, over burlap, as shown on pattern.

OWL: Lay tissue pattern over burlap on panel. Push in some blued nails along head and tail to hold pattern in position. Using the blued nails, push through tissue, through burlap, into the styrofoam. Do not push all the way in, allowing head of nail to remain ½″ to ⅜″ above surface. Outline the wing and head areas and tail. For feet, push the gold upholstery tacks through the braid into the styrofoam.

FLOWERS: Push in a black map tack. Five white map tacks circling it make petals.

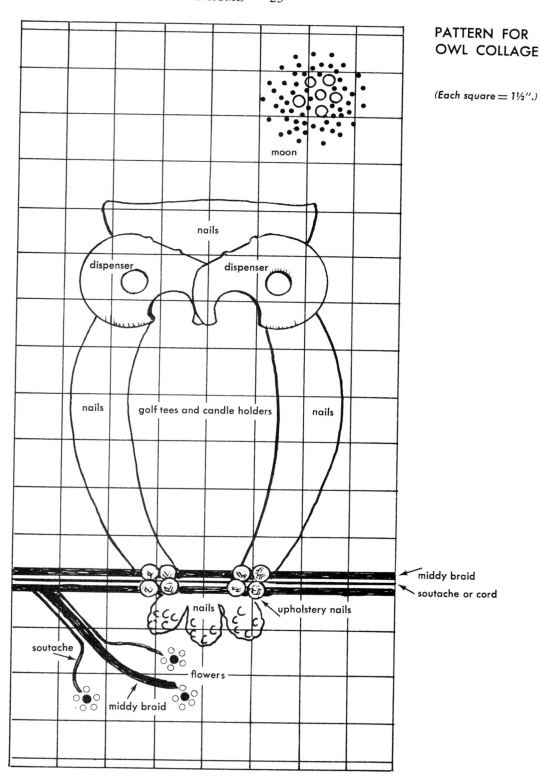

PATTERN FOR
OWL COLLAGE

(Each square = 1½".)

moon

nails

dispenser   dispenser

nails   golf tees and candle holders   nails

middy braid
soutache or cord

nails   upholstery nails

soutache

flowers

middy braid

MOON: Push in white thumbtacks as indicated by the open circles. Push in white map tacks at dots.

Remove tissue pattern, pulling and tearing it away. Remove any small pieces with tweezers. Fill in the wings and head with the blued nails. These should be close with nail heads not quite touching.

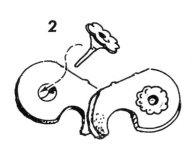

BEAK AND EYES: Open the plastic dispenser and remove the metal cutting edge and roller. If dispensers are transparent, spray-paint the inside of each white. Spray gold very lightly on the outside, mostly the beak area (Fig. 1). Overlap points to form beak at angle shown in pattern. Glue together. Add glue to edges of dispenser, place on picture. Add glue to tips of two candle holders, and push down through hole in each dispenser into styrofoam, to hold plastic pieces in place (Fig. 2). Glue black bead in center of each candle holder for eyes.

Now fill in chest area with yellow and white golf tees and the remaining birthday-candle holders. Use them in whatever proportion you have available. Tops should be about ½" above surface. Intersperse units of yellow and white to make chest area attractive. Place units close but not touching. Add a dab of glue to centers of candle holders, and glue a white bead in the center of each (Fig. 3).

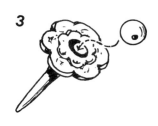

TO FINISH: Attach frame. Place styrofoam glue along edge of styrofoam sheet, top and bottom. Glue on the first yardstick piece so it lines up with back and protrudes in front about ½". Gently hammer in two small nails to hold while glue dries. Glue and nail on yardstick for opposite end. Glue sides in place. Glue corners, nail together (Fig. 4). Attach a screw-on type hanger at top.

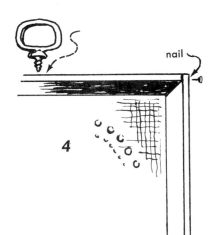

nail

HANG on wall after glue is thoroughly dry. Of course this should be hung well out of the reach of children who could dismantle the picture as easily as you put it together. A tiny dab of styrofoam glue at the tip of each nail (or other unit), as it is inserted, could make it more permanent, but this is not necessary.

VARIATIONS

Instead of an owl, find an attractive print about 5" × 7" (or size desired) and mount it in this type of frame (Fig. 5). The one shown is a print of a Rembrandt etching.

Cut backing of styrofoam and the burlap covering to size needed for print, allowing 2" to 3" burlap to show around the print on all sides (see Fig. 5). Attach burlap to backing.

Cut a piece of heavy cardboard or masonite the size of the print plus
.¼" extra all around. Paint yardstick and masonite black. Allow to dry.
Glue print to masonite panel. Apply several coats of varnish.

Attach yardsticks to styrofoam as before. Glue four golf tees to back
of mounted picture, about 1" from each corner (Fig. 6). When dry, add
glue to tips of tees and poke into styrofoam, centering picture. This creates
a panel that is raised from the background about ½".

TO FINISH: Screw hanger to top.

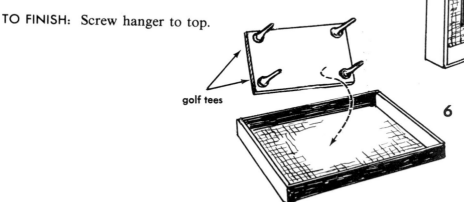

golf tees

CLIPBOARD

There are countless ways to decorate and personalize clipboards, so each
will be unique, regardless of the number you make. By varying colors and
trims, you can make a board suitable for a den, a game room, or a child's
room.

MATERIALS NEEDED
9" × 12" clipboard from variety or stationery store
1½ yds. soutache or middy braid (optional)
6½" × 9" to 8" × 10" picture of appropriate subject, and small
    print about 1" wide. (Sources: prints, magazines, calendars,
    brochures)
Latex paint
Varnish, matte finish
14" piece of string or cord
Pencil
White glue
Epoxy glue or household cement (for metal)
Also needed: ¾" thick book or wood block, soft dry cloth, twine,
    brushes for varnish and paint

*See color photograph
facing page 41.*

PREPARE BOARD: So you can paint the entire board neatly, the clip should be held open while you are working. Slip sturdy object or block about ¾" thick under clip. Through holes in top of clip, *securely* tie it in *open* position with strong twine. Remove block. Paint the board, front and back. Allow to dry.

SELECT AN APPROPRIATE PICTURE: For kitchens, prints of flowers or fruit are usually popular. If you prefer, cut out separate pieces, representing fruits or vegetables, and group them.

ATTACH PRINT: Spread a thin layer of white glue over back of print. Thin glue with water if it doesn't spread easily (about the consistency of light cream). Apply print to board slightly below center. Working out from the center, with a soft, clean cloth, rub down print to smooth out wrinkles or bubbles. A damp cloth will remove any excess glue.

ADD EDGING (optional): If print is small or a border is needed for accent, glue on soutache or middy braid. All around board, draw a line about ¼" inside edge. Lay a line of white glue along line. To glue on edging, start at clip top. Keep a damp cloth handy to clean hands and remove excess glue. If picture is large enough, edging could be glued along border of picture.

TO DECORATE CLIP: Paint the clip if desired, or leave in natural metal color. Find a picture about 1" wide that blends well with your print, to fit the blank space on center of clip (or to cover the brand name there). Cut it out. Using epoxy, glue small print onto the clip (Fig. 1). To decorate edge of clip, cut braid about ½" longer than needed. Glue to edge of clip, then fold ends around to back and glue.

TO FINISH: When all glue is dry, apply several coats of clear varnish or plastic finish to clipboard and clip decoration. When thoroughly dry, remove twine that is holding the clip open. Slip a few pieces of paper under the clip for notes.

TIE a 14" piece of cord to a pencil and tie other end to the clip.

VARIATIONS

Use a large print that covers the entire board, or use gift-wrap paper with suitable design. Cut-off edges can be used to cover much of the clip. Glue on edging as needed to accent clip.

You can also decorate the clip by covering it with felt. Choose a color that complements the picture to be glued on board. Make a paper pattern by tracing contour of clip and adding ¼" all around. Cut shape out of felt. Using top of pattern, cut a small shape for back of clip top (Fig. 2). Sew around curve and slip over top of clip (clipboard can hang by other hole). Trace a motif from the print used and cut this out of felt. Or cut any appropriate shapes of contrasting felt (Fig. 3). Glue felt covering to clip, using fabric glue that adheres to metal (check the label). Trim even with edges. Glue felt design in center front. Add edging, if needed.

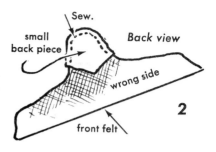

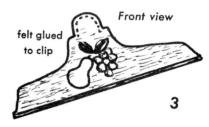

RECIPE HOLDER

This tiny shelf ornament holds a recipe in the kitchen or a reminder note on a desk. Whatever decorates the base determines its character. For a cool, contemporary look, marbles give dimension and color.

MATERIALS NEEDED
Metal salad fork
2½" to 2¾" diameter twist-on type jar top
Epoxy putty (stick type), clear epoxy glue
16 silver beads about ⅛" diameter (or silver cake decorations)
2 sewing-machine bobbins (the kind with several holes)
4 blue marbles (about ¾" diameter)
2 silver (or blue) beads about ½" diameter
Also needed: Sandpaper (very fine), steel wool, pliers (or vise)

SELECT A FORK from discards or buy an inexpensive one in a variety store. The cheaper the metal, the easier it is to bend. Using pliers (or a vise if necessary), bend fork into shape shown (Fig. 1). Make horizontal surface as flat as possible. Bend two center tines slightly forward.

TO MAKE BASE: A plain-colored jar top can be used. Merely sandpaper center where fork is to be attached. The putty will adhere only to

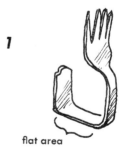

flat area

raw metal. If there is printing on the cover, or if you wish a silver-color base to match the fork, sand jar top until most of the paint is gone. Finish polishing with dry steel wool.

TO ATTACH FORK TO BASE: Mix a very small amount of putty. Place a strip of putty on the base. Push fork down firmly into the putty (Fig. 2). Remove any excess, so putty is even with edge of fork. Allow putty to dry until very hard.

TO ADD DECORATIONS TO BOBBINS: Using clear epoxy (or household cement), glue on four silver beads, placing in holes shown (Fig. 3). Glue four more beads in the holes directly below on bobbin. Glue a ½″ bead in center hole of the bobbin. Repeat on other bobbin. Allow to dry thoroughly.

Mix a small amount of the epoxy, and set bobbin on its edge at one side of fork base. With a toothpick, glue all contact points of bobbin, base and fork. Prop into position. Repeat, gluing other bobbin on opposite side of fork (Fig. 4). Let dry.

TO ATTACH MARBLES: Mix another small amount of epoxy. Glue one marble in front of each bobbin, adding glue where marbles touch fork, base, and bobbin. When firmly set, glue another marble to center front, (Fig. 5) and one marble to back near bent-up end of fork.

PLACE A RECIPE CARD in tines after all glue is thoroughly dry. Check to see that card sets at a convenient angle. If not, bend fork tines slightly to adjust.

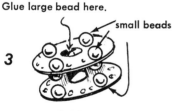

2

putty

Glue large bead here.

3

small beads

bobbin

4

Glue on decorated bobbin.

area to glue on marble

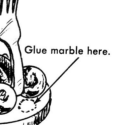

5

Glue marble on back.

Glue marble here.

VARIATIONS

If fork is badly worn, parts or all of the note holder may be painted. Fake or dried flowers, or tiny figurines, can be used to decorate the base. Natural elements—rocks, crystals, shells, driftwood—are equally attractive for decorations.

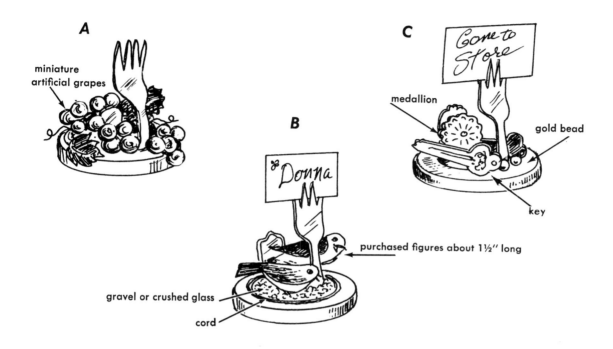

Here are three other ideas for trimming the holder, after the fork has been glued to the base:

A) Spray-paint unit light green and rub on silver highlights. Glue on miniature artificial fruit or vegetable clusters.

B) Paint center of base over horizontal section of fork as far as ridge of jar top. Glue silver cord around edge of painted area. Fill this area with white glue and sprinkle crushed glass (or aquarium gravel) onto it. Work pieces down into the glue. Add more glue, if necessary, to secure them. Glue on a small bird, mushroom, or other figure.

C) Using bright colors, spray-paint entire unit. Also spray-paint two or three old keys a vibrant gold (or buy key blanks). With epoxy, glue a key on each side of fork. Glue third key (or decorative medallion from jewelry) at center back.

EASTER EGGS AND TREE

Hand decoration of eggs at Eastertime is a family tradition in many homes. Some people use methods handed down for generations. Others like to try new ideas each year. After the eggs are decorated, an Easter tree makes a charming way to display the eggs and accent a holiday table.

PLASTIC EGGS

Those that open can be transformed into attractive decorations sturdy enough for children and glamorous enough to appeal to adults.

See color photograph facing page 137.

MATERIALS NEEDED
Plastic egg
Gold spray
Gold foil motifs (or gold doilies)
Gold cord (from gift wrap)
Various beads, ribbons, edgings, or trims
Fabric glue
Also needed: Single-edged razor blade, egg carton

PREPARE EGG: To tone down the often garish color of the plastic, spray the egg lightly with gold. Hold spray can about two feet away, allowing just a light mist of gold to fall on the egg, so it retains its original color underneath.

GLUE TRIM around center. Choose fabric ribbon or stretch lace. Glue other trims or plastic beading along edges of ribbon or lace. Ease trims around. Do part of a row. Prop up in egg carton while glue dries, then finish row. It will be easier to butt ends (see page 11) after part of trim is dry and firm. Overlap ends slightly and cut with single-edged razor blade.

ENDS: Glue gold-foil medallion or other round motif (Fig. 1) on bottom end. For hanging, cut gold or silver cord 6″ long. Make a small hole in center of a lace or foil medallion. Put ends of cord through; then glue to top end of egg (Fig. 2). Scatter small round motifs on undecorated parts.

FOR A SPECIAL TOUCH, you can add a tiny nylon butterfly, available at a craft store. The wire of the butterfly should be glued under the center band of decoration.

1

foil motif →

2

REAL EGG SHELLS

These are always fun to decorate at Eastertime and can be trimmed as prettily as the plastic ones described above. Tint shells with food coloring, then add the trims.

Or you can make open scenic eggs from real eggshell.

MATERIALS NEEDED
Eggshell
Yellow-green variegated (Madras) tissue (about ½" wide)
4" decorative ribbon (about ¼" wide)
7" string small plastic beads
7" string flat-back pearls
7" yellow baby rickrack
4" gold cord
¾" bunny or chicken, small artificial flowers
Also needed: White glue, tweezers

PREPARE REAL EGGSHELL: Cut a small hole (½" or so) in the side of a raw egg, then shake inside of egg out of this hole. Wash and dry shell thoroughly. (Have extra shells available to allow for breakage.)

Tear small pieces of colored tissue paper (about ½" square). Cover outside of egg by gluing on paper pieces with thinned white glue. Glue on a single layer of tissue, overlapping edges at angles. This will strengthen the eggshell and give it color. With small scissors, enlarge hole to shape shown (Fig. 1). Cover inside of shell with pieces of the colored tissue.

1

TRIM: Glue rickrack around opening on the inside and glue bead trim around outside of opening to hide any irregularities. For hanging cord, pull piece of cord through end of ribbon or foil trim. Glue to top of egg, then down center back (Fig. 2). Glue another row of trim around opening to hide ends of back trim. (For this row, flat-backed pearls are good.)

2

cord   Glue down.

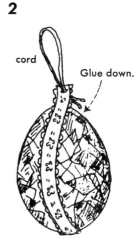

Back view

DECORATE INSIDE of eggshell. Glue tiny artificial leaves and flowers at back of shell. Use tweezers to help make the arrangement. Allow room for a figure in front. When glue has set, position a small, appropriate figure such as a bunny, mouse, bird, or butterfly, and glue it in place. Bend leaves slightly if necessary to make scene attractive.

EASTER TREE

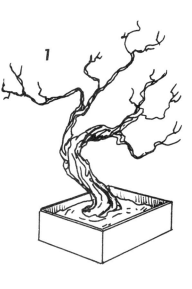

MATERIALS NEEDED
Cardboard box
Plaster of Paris
Driftwood or tree branch
Green paint
Easter decorations

SMALL TREE: Place a small branch (or driftwood piece) in sturdy cardboard box (Fig. 1). Prop branch into position. Fill container about 2″ deep with plaster of Paris (see package for mixing). After plaster sets, remove container. When it dries, paint base green.

OR MAKE A LARGE TREE to display eggs for sale at a bazaar. Find a large, sturdy, dry branch. Make plaster (or cement) base large enough to support it. Decorate base with greenery and artificial flowers.

DECORATE TREES with Easter eggs. Add flour-clay ornaments cut with cooky cutters (Fig. 2). (See directions for flour-clay decorations on opposite page.) Make bunnies, chickens, flowers, and butterflies. Paint them in pastel colors.

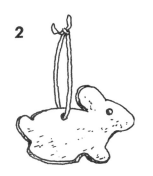

Styrofoam eggs are colorful and easy to decorate. Trims, sequins, ribbons, and beads can be applied with pins sold for this purpose. If you make eggs for children, it is safer to glue on trims.

CHRISTMAS ORNAMENTS OF FLOUR CLAY

Cooky-type ornaments can be made with flour clay. Although they look edible, they are not, and may be used for many years as permanent Christmas-tree trinkets. Left in natural color, they resemble real cookies, but you can transform them into exotic decorations with paint or gilt and various trims. See color photograph facing page 137.

MATERIALS NEEDED

Flour clay:

    4 cups all-purpose flour

    2 cups salt

    1 teaspoon powdered alum

    1½ cups water

Plastic-based poster or acrylic paint

Spray-on finish (varnish or plastic)

Clear shellac (optional)

Trims, glitter, jewels, gold cord, wire, etc.

Also needed: Food coloring (optional), cooky cutters, plastic straw, fine wire, baking sheet, fine sandpaper, wax paper

TO MAKE CLAY: Mix all ingredients thoroughly with hands. (If dough is too dry, work in 1 tablespoon water.) Dough can be colored by dividing into several parts and kneading desired food coloring into each part. Roll or mold as directed.

TO ROLL FLAT ORNAMENTS: On lightly floured board, roll dough ⅛" thick. Cut with cooky cutters. If ornaments are to be hung, make a hole in each ¼" from top, using end of plastic straw like a cutter.

TO MOLD DIMENSIONAL ORNAMENTS: Shape dough no more than ½" thick into forms of flowers, fruits, vegetables, or animals. For hanging, insert fine wire in top of each ornament.

Note: Remaining dough can be kept in plastic wrap or aluminum foil and refrigerated for about 2 weeks.

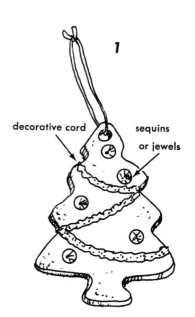

decorative cord   sequins or jewels

BAKE: Heat oven to 250°. Place ornaments on ungreased baking sheet. Bake *about 30 minutes.* Remove from oven, then turn over (if possible) and bake *about 1½ hours longer* (1 hour for ⅛" thick ornaments) or until completely hard and dry. Remove from baking sheet. Cool.

TO FINISH: When cool, smooth lightly with fine sandpaper. Outline designs on ornaments with pencil. Coat with paint. (Remember to paint sides and backs of ornaments.) When dry, spray ornaments with clear plastic (polyurethane) or varnish to finish. You may prefer to brush ornaments with clear shellac.

If wire was not previously inserted, cut a 5″ piece of gold or silver gift-wrap cord. Slip through top hole and tie for a hanger.

VARIATIONS
Jewels, glitter, and trims can be glued on after ornaments are painted (Fig. 1).

FOR A WREATH,   use a round cooky cutter and cut out center with a bottle top. Tie a tiny bow of red soutache braid. Glue in place (Fig. 2). Add trims.

FOR ROCKING HORSE, roll snakes of clay and lay onto cut-out shape, forming saddle and bridle. Roll a tiny ball for eye (Fig. 3). When baked, paint the reins, saddle, and rockers red. Add glitter.

ANGEL: This clay can also be used to make ornaments similar to the peasant art of "bread dough" figures. Cut a basic shape with cooky cutter (such as this angel) or cut a shape from rolled-out dough with knife. For face, roll a ball of clay, and flatten slightly against background shape. Roll snake-like pieces of dough and lay on, curving to form outlines of shapes (Fig. 4). The angel's hair and dress hem are made this way.

Take tiny bits of dough, roll between fingers, flatten or shape, lay on basic shape. These lumps can be overlapped to achieve a quality of texture and dimension (see wings). Push and dent with a tool for more texture. When baked, the figures are charming, even in natural dough color. If desired, however, they can be painted in bright peasant colors. Observe native crafts and let them inspire you to make your own flour-clay figures.

2

green glitter   red beads

3

red glitter

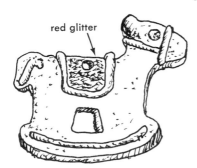

4

ANGEL ORNAMENTS

You can transform a discard into a novel tree ornament featuring an angel or other Yuletide figure. These baubles will vary, depending on the size and shape of the plastic blister you work with. (Many different items are sold in blister packages.) Remove the blister carefully from its cardboard backing, for this transparent shape is the basic part of your finished ornament.

MATERIALS NEEDED
(*for oval ornament*)
4½" oval plastic blister (this one covered a hair barrette). Use whatever size is available.
12" decorative gold edging
12" string of beads (sold by the yard)
Foil gift-wrap paper (or old Christmas card) for background
3" × 6" plain cardboard (from cereal box or back of a writing pad)
3" × 6" gold cardboard (from old Christmas card)
Scrap green tinsel
2" gold plastic angel (from craft shop or variety stores at Christmas time)
3 fake jewels, flat-back
4" narrow gold cord
Fabric glue
(*for rectangular ornament*) Similar materials—except size, shape and colors vary.

See color photograph facing page 137.

The oval ornament shown here was made from a blister about ¼" deep at the center. An angel was chosen that would fit well inside, but any appropriate figure can be used.

BACKGROUND: Select a piece of foil gift-wrap paper, one with a small design or of a solid color. Backgrounds cut from old Christmas cards are also very effective. (Some embossed cards have scenes that can be used without adding a figure in front. Use the blister to frame the scene.)

TO MOUNT THE BACKGROUND: Cut a piece (from paper or card) slightly larger than the blister shape and glue it to the piece of cardboard. Trace around blister shape on the paper background. Establish position

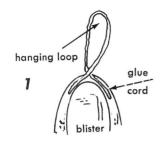

1

hanging loop

glue

cord

blister

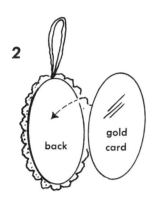

2

back

gold card

3

motif

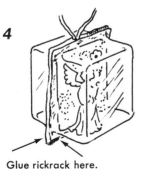

4

Glue rickrack here.

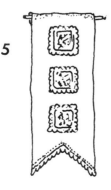

5

of the figure and other decorations. Place blister over them to check fit and appearance. When arrangement is satisfactory, glue all items in position on the paper. In the oval illustrated here, green tinsel was glued beneath the angel's feet, and three jewels above her.

After all items are secured, glue edges of blister to the paper. When dry, trim excess backing close to blister edge.

FOR GOLD BACKING: Make pattern by tracing shape of blister on paper and adding about $1/16''$ all around. Then cut out backing from gold cardboard or foil wrapping paper. Set aside.

FOR HANGING LOOP: Fold 4" gold cord in half, and glue about 1" of each end of cord to lip of blister on top (Fig. 1).

TO FINISH EDGE: Glue gold fabric edging around edge of blister in front (over ends of hanging cord). Allow edging to protrude ¼" or less over edge all around. Glue on a little at a time, starting at center top. As glue gets tacky, adjust edging into position. Overlap slightly at top where ends meet.

Trimmings and edgings should be as lavish as possible. (They also hide the glued-down unsightly part of the blister.) If desired, add a row of plastic beads around oval, next to and over edging. Complete by gluing gold oval backing to back of cardboard (Fig. 2).

THE RECTANGULAR ORNAMENT is the same except that it is smaller and doubled-sided. Use two identical-sized plastic blisters about ½" deep (the kind that are used to pack small items—screws, pins, sequins, etc.). For each unit, place a 1¼" angel against a background of green foil paper. Cut a ¼" motif from a gold paper doily. Place above the angel. In the center of the motif, glue a jewel (Fig. 3). After gluing in all parts and gluing blisters in place on each unit, trim cardboard backs to size. Glue hanging cord to back of one unit. Then glue two units together, back to back (Fig. 4). When dry, glue gold rickrack around edges on both sides.

VARIATIONS

The shape of the blister you choose will give you ideas for your own decorations. The two described are merely suggestions. A group of large blisters can be made into a wall hanging (glue to felt backing) or pennant (Fig. 5). Use tiny ones for package ornaments. Blister Christmas tree ornaments are durable, so can be used year after year.

EMBOSSED FOIL ANGEL

Here is an angel that might well be your most effective Christmas decoration when placed in an entrance hall or set on a mantel. By adding a silvery three-panel screen (see variations), this decoration could be the focal point of a Christmas bazaar. If you already have a favorite figurine, make only the screen to serve as an elegant background for the sculpture or grouping.

See color photograph
facing page 40.

MATERIALS NEEDED
6 pieces of corrugated cardboard about 18″ long, 6″ to 13″ wide (from sides of cartons or from any supply store)
3″ diameter styrofoam ball
4 hatpins or corsage pins (1 at least 1¾″ long)
1 candle about 1″ diameter, 5½″ long
1 plastic pill bottle about 1¼″ diameter, 2″ high
3 long pipe cleaners
2 round plastic doilies 12″ and 9″ diameter (also 1 oval doily, optional)
1 yard decorative cotton edging
Silver gift-wrap cord (or tinsel)
1 stainless steel pot scrubber
Lightweight aluminum foil
2 ice-cream sticks
2 brass paper fasteners (1″ long)
Walnut stain (or brown paste shoe polish)
Rubber cement
Fabric glue
Also needed: Brush for stain, 1½″ masking tape, mat knife, small knife, soft cloth, rag, metal-edged ruler, compass, awl, lightweight paper for patterns, newspaper

ENLARGE PATTERNS on paper. (See page 38.) Draw wing on folded paper, trace other side, open. Trace patterns onto corrugated cardboard. Trace lower part of sleeve from enlarged pattern. Draw two lower sleeves on the cardboard.

BODY: See the diagrams on page 39 for dimensions. Each piece is a triangle. (Draw directly on the cardboard if you wish.) Measure base and center line which must be perpendicular to the base. Draw in each triangle side by connecting ends of base line to center top point. For back, measure

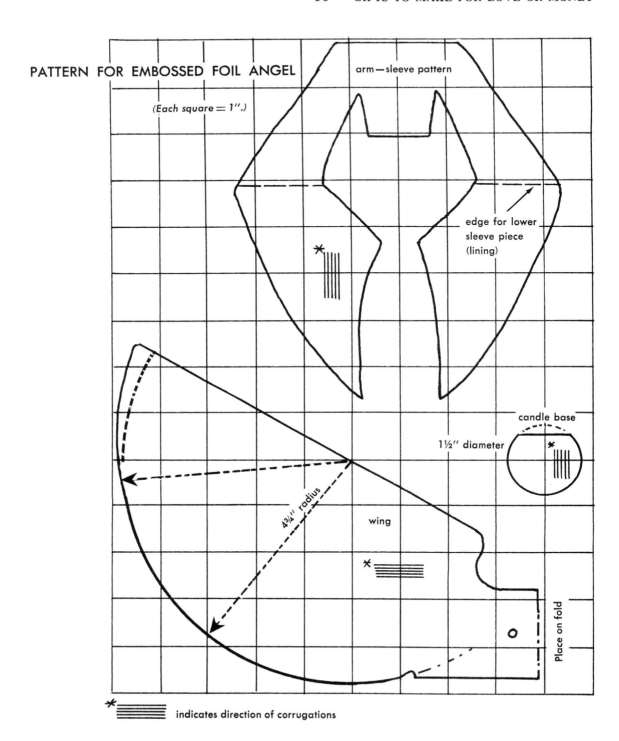

PATTERN FOR EMBOSSED FOIL ANGEL

(Each square = 1".)

arm—sleeve pattern

edge for lower
sleeve piece
(lining)

candle base

1½" diameter

4¾" radius

wing

Place on fold

*≣≣≣ indicates direction of corrugations

DIAGRAMS OF BODY PIECES

Diagrams are ¼ actual size.

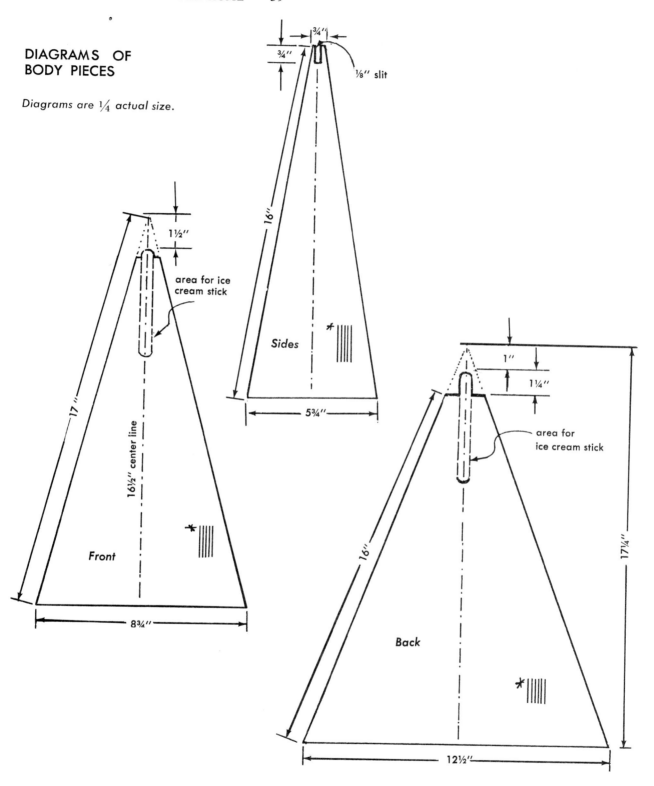

¾″

¾″

⅛″ slit

1½″

area for ice cream stick

17″

16½″ center line

Front

8¾″

16″

Sides

5¾″

1″

1¼″

area for ice cream stick

16″

17¼″

Back

12½″

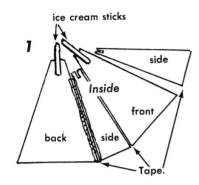

ice cream sticks

1

side

Inside

front

back   side

Tape.

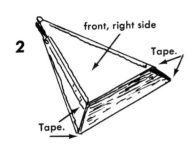

2

front, right side

Tape.

Tape.

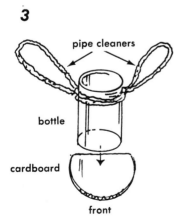

3

pipe cleaners

bottle

cardboard

front

1″ down from tip of triangle. Lay ice cream stick in place, draw around tip, remove. Measure down 1¼″ and draw top edge either side of stick area. (See diagrams of body pieces.)

SIDE PIECES: Draw slit ¾″ deep, ⅛″ wide as shown. Draw one front, one back, and two side pieces on the board, with corrugations going up and down, if possible. Draw a 1½″ circle, cut one side straight (see pattern).

CUT OUT all straight-edge pieces using the mat knife and a metal-edged ruler. Place each piece on scrap cardboard when cutting.

TO ASSEMBLE: Glue ice-cream sticks to inside at top of front and back pieces, in position shown on cutting diagrams. Attach sides and front body piece on inside, using masking tape. Tape one edge of back to edge of side (Fig. 1), turn over. Fold up, so edges align properly at base, and tape along all joinings (Fig. 2) to complete body.

For arms and candle, wind two pipe cleaners around pill bottle (Fig. 3), leaving about 1½″ loop on each side. Twist in ends to secure. Lay bottle between sleeve ends. Apply glue between sleeve and lining piece on each end, sandwiching pipe-cleaner loops between cardboard pieces (Fig. 4). Glue circle to base of pill bottle, flat side at back (see Fig. 3). Add glue to pipe cleaners around bottle to make more secure. Allow to dry.

TO ADD DECORATIVE TEXTURES: To create effect of embossing, use plastic doilies and fabric edgings. Select edgings that are firm and have considerable depth. Other firm, open textures can be used, such as sections of plastic berry baskets, cord, rope, string, etc.

Using fabric glue, attach edging about 1″ up from bottom edges of side pieces. Glue a triangular shape in center front, with point about 8″ up from base (Fig 5). Glue a piece of edging around candle-holder base above cardboard piece.

For texture on wings, cut a 9″ doily in half and glue one half to each wing. For skirt, cut a motif about 4″ across from the center of the doily. From the side of the oval doily, cut a motif to fit along edges of sleeves (or glue on fabric edging). Cut a piece from left-over piece of doily to fit on upper chest.

With rubber cement, coat all cardboard surfaces and back of doily pieces. Allow to dry. Place all pieces in position as planned. Trim off any excess of doily piece at inner edge of wings.

Embossed
Foil
Angel (page 37)

Clipboard (page 25); Oshibana Stationery (page 48); Pottery-like Vase (page 12); Candlestick (page 16); Coasters (page 11)

HEAD: Whittle out area of styrofoam ball to accommodate the ice cream stick ends. Head should be set about ¾" down on sticks.

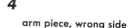

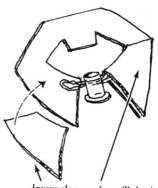

arm piece, wrong side

lower sleeve piece (lining)

COVERING: All corrugated pieces and the head should be completely covered with foil. Tear off a square of foil large enough to handle comfortably. Crumple up, then gently uncrumple it — just enough to make it lie flat. Apply a coat of rubber cement to dull side of foil. Add coat of cement over glued-on doily pieces and edgings. When dry, gently lay on the foil. With a soft cloth (an old washcloth will do), work foil around decorative motifs. Soon their contours will appear in relief. Rub other areas to make sure foil is firmly attached to cardboard. This creates a wrinkled, faceted surface.

Crumple another piece of foil, flatten it, coat dull side with cement. Add cement along edges of the piece of foil already in place. When dry, add new foil piece, overlapping edges slightly. Continue until all surfaces, decorations, and edges of cardboard are covered. Foil pieces can be any size, just be sure there is always a layer of cement on both surfaces before attaching, or edges may pick up. Fold foil around bottom edge of skirt and inside about 1". Leave ¾" ends of ice-cream sticks at neck uncovered.

Test to see how candle fits bottle. Add extra layer of foil inside if it is too loose. Remove candle. Cover arms, candle holder, and any part of pipe cleaners that show with foil. Cover styrofoam ball, working crumpled foil completely around it.

Rub all foil coverings thoroughly to bring out design, and to make sure they adhere firmly. This will also remove any traces of rubber cement that remain on the surface.

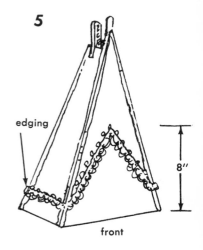

edging

front

8"

TO COLOR: Brush stain (or apply shoe polish) on all foil areas. Allow to dry slightly. Remove excess with rag. As it dries, rub with a soft cloth to accentuate the textural designs.

TO COMPLETE: Place wings in position at back with base of wings about 12½" up from bottom edge. With an awl, make two holes through wings and body. Insert paper fasteners, open up inside. (This type of attachment allows wings to be removed for storage when the holiday season is over.)

Slide arm piece (with candle) down in side slits, bend slightly at shoulders to bring candle holder forward at proper angle. To secure candle in upright position, insert the hat pin horizontally through the cardboard base of the candle and into the body. Wind tip of pin with masking tape (or add a small cork to tip) to prevent sharp tip from scratching.

6

bead

pin

assembled

7

Pin at center top.

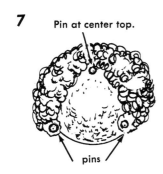

pins

HAIR: Open up pot scrubber, slip over head. Shape around head to fit like hair. Use corsage pins to hold or slip a straight pin through a small bead (Fig. 6). Arrange hair line as desired (Fig. 7). For halo, wind a pipe cleaner with silver or tinsel gift-wrap cord, gluing as you wind. Insert in head in proper position. Add glue on cardboard and sticks at neck. Insert sticks in whittled out area at bottom of head. Add a silver cord tie around neck, or glue on more aluminum foil if there are any unfinished areas showing. Slip candle in its holder.

8

center point

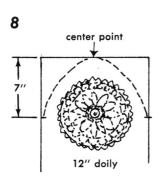

7"

12" doily

VARIATIONS

The candle is for effect only and should not be lighted. Although the foil makes the figure non-flammable, the heat would melt the styrofoam. If you prefer, this angel can hold a decorative bell, a ball, a flower, a book, or a small (5" to 7") decorative Christmas tree. Just wind pipe cleaners around base and glue in position.

If you prefer more color, parts of skirt or arms can be covered with colored foil, the kind florists use to wrap around flower pots.

An impressive screen can be made by the same method and is an attractive backgound for the angel or for any figure or crèche grouping.

9

Tape.

THREE-PANEL SCREEN: Cut two corrugated pieces 28" × 13½" with corrugations running up and down. Place a 12" plastic doily near top center of one piece. Mark area around top half of doily to center point of top of cardboard piece. Draw curve (Fig. 8). On paper, trace curve and turn over to make curve on other side of top. Cut out. Trace curve on other cardboard piece and cut out. Glue a 12" doily on each piece. Cut one piece in half vertically. Place the three sections together as shown (Fig. 9) and tape. Fold sides together over front and tape joinings in back. Open flat.

Using fabric glue, attach string or cord about ¼" in from all edges. Add on more textures if you wish but these are sufficient. Cover with foil, stain, and rub highlights.

You can also make a four-panel screen in the same way. Just cut four pieces instead of two. If you want to use the screen as a background for a figure already made or for a flower arrangement, adjust size to fit.

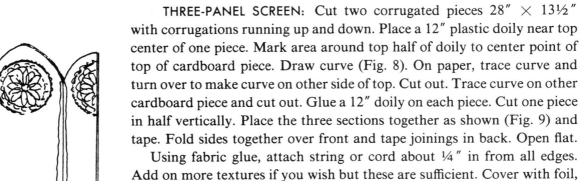

DANCING SANTA STOCKING

Make a loved child a stocking of his own to be filled with gifts and goodies. Very likely it will be unpacked many Christmases thereafter and serve as a nostalgic reminder of past holidays.

MATERIALS NEEDED

$\frac{1}{3}$ yd. green velour (or felt, velveteen, or heavy green cotton fabric), 40″ wide

3″ × 22″ piece white fake fur

6″ square bright pink felt

1″ × 2″ pale pink felt (or fabric)

3″ × 6″ black felt (or scraps)

2 black buttons, ¼″ in diameter (optional)

½″ square scrap of red felt (optional)

8″ white cord or ribbon

¼″ diameter red bead or button (or ¼″ circle red felt)

1 jingle bell; 1 smaller jingle bell (optional)

3 yds. (approximately) white ball fringe with ¾″ pompon balls. (Fringes vary considerably as to number of balls per yard. ½ yard of fringe is needed for top of stocking. Besides that you will need 28 or 29 balls for Santa's trim.)

Fabric glue (if desired)

STOCKING: Enlarge pattern (page 45) on paper. Draw Santa in place. This will serve as a guide later for positioning pieces. Lay pattern for stocking on folded green fabric. Cut two (Fig. 1).

TOP CUFF: Cut a piece of fake fur 3″ × 17″.

SANTA: Trace Santa sections from the enlarged drawing. Trace each Santa piece (hat, body, feet, hands, and face) on separate pieces of paper. Cut hat and body of deep pink felt; face, of light pink felt. Cut mittens and feet of black felt. Make pattern for beard by tracing shape in Fig. 2. Cut beard of white fake fur. If you want to add a mouth, trace and cut it out of red felt. Trace eyes and cut out of black felt (or use buttons).

TO ASSEMBLE SANTA: Pin pieces in position on front green stocking piece. (Set aside back stocking piece.) Neatly appliqué all pieces in

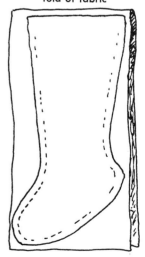

fold of fabric

1

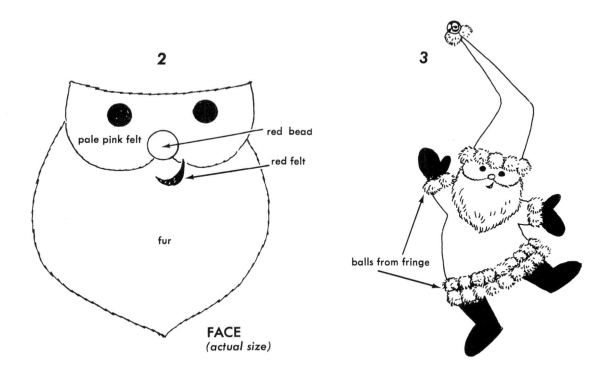

2

pale pink felt

red bead

red felt

fur

FACE
(actual size)

3

balls from fringe

position by hand or machine (or glue on). Sew beard over top of body, matching top of beard to bottom of face (Fig. 2). Place features as shown (Fig. 2). Sew on (or glue) black felt eyes (or sew on buttons). If mouth is to be added, clip fur around mouth area to make room for it. Sew or glue mouth in position. Sew on red bead, or button, or red felt circle for nose.

TO TRIM SANTA'S SUIT: Remove balls from fringe. Balls have a small metal clip to hold them together. Sew up through this clip and down into fabric. Sew a row along bottom edge of coat, about 9 balls across. Sew another row of balls above this one. Sew 2 balls at edge of each sleeve. Sew a row of 5 balls along edge of hat. Sew 2 balls and the small jingle bell at the tip of the cap (or use 3 balls). Santa is complete (Fig. 3).

TO MAKE STOCKING: Lay green stocking pieces with right sides together, Santa inside. Pin (baste, if desired) and sew around by machine, making ⅜″ seam. Leave top open. Turn right side out.

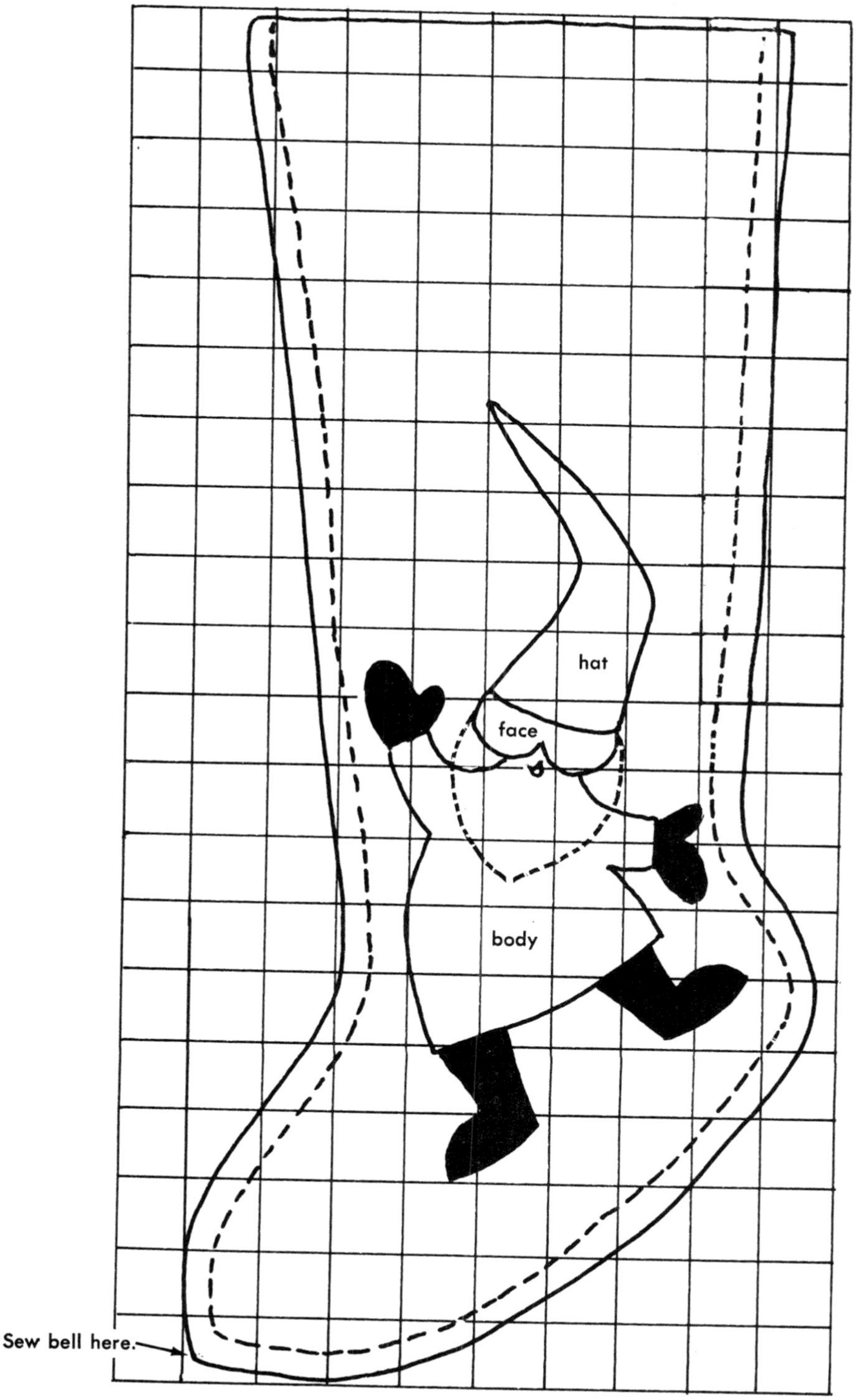

PATTERN FOR DANCING SANTA STOCKING

(Each square = 1".)

hat

face

body

Sew bell here.

Dotted line indicates ⅜" seam allowance all around.

4

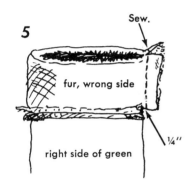

Leave seam allowance of fur.

wrong side of fur

right side of green

CUFF: Circle inside top of stocking with strip of fake fur, setting fur side against wrong side of the green material (Fig. 4). Baste top edges together. Machine-stitch around top, making ¼″ seam. Bring fur out of stocking and sew side seam of fur by hand (Fig. 5), allowing about ¼″ beyond stocking for fold-over. Turn cuff over on outside of stocking. Hand-sew ball-fringe edging to fur, covering raw edge (Fig. 6).

HANGING LOOP: Fold cord (or ribbon) in half. Sew ends ½″ down inside of stocking at side seam of cuff. Sew large bell at tip of toe.

VARIATIONS

A Santa wall hanging can also be made by enlarging the pattern of Santa, making each square 2″. For background, use a 16″ × 26″ panel of green felt. Cut pieces to make Santa. (Larger amount of felt is needed for making wall-hanging Santa.) Use dotted line on pattern to get shape of beard. Cut from fake fur.

If fabric is used for background instead of felt, sew a ½″ hem all around before attaching Santa pieces. Glue these pieces to backing. Use a larger ball fringe with 1″ pompons. Sew in place. Glue some pink or white fringe to the bottom edge of the panel (Fig. 7). Tack on wall or door.

5

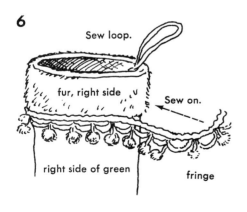

Sew.

fur, wrong side

right side of green

¼″

6

Sew loop.

fur, right side

Sew on.

right side of green

fringe

7

3. GIFTS WOMEN LOVE

For most women, a personal, handcrafted token of affection is a truly refreshing change from the usual commercial gift. Many of the gifts described in the second chapter of this book should be very appealing to a young homemaker. Some ideas in the section for teens may please her, too.

Attractive, exotic jewelry can often solve many a gift problem, and designing jewelry is not as difficult as one might think. In Chapter 7, the clay and hardware pieces intended for teen-agers can be easily adapted for women by using more sophisticated shapes and more subtle colors. For instance, the hinge belt on velvet (page 131) would make a suitable gift for a young woman. Also, a variation of the glass paperweight, box, or desk set described in the chapter on gifts for men would be equally appropriate on a feminine desk.

Throughout this book you will find basic gift ideas that can be restyled for women, but the following section is devoted exclusively to them.

OSHIBANA STATIONERY

*See color photograph
facing page 41.*

The Japanese, with their special flair for enhancing the beauty of nature, have developed a technique for preserving natural flowers between sheets of rice paper. This process, called Oshibana, has inspired an American version that employs everyday materials.

MATERIALS NEEDED

Facial tissues (select a good brand, even textured, that becomes semitransparent when glue is applied)

Wax paper

White glue

Assortment of natural materials: dried flowers, weeds, ferns, leaves, etc., pressed butterflies (optional)

Purchased stationery, plain, in pastel colors, single-fold, about 4″ × 5½″. (Some stores carry stationery pads in various sizes with envelopes to match.) Use any size you want. Adjust instructions accordingly.

Also needed: Soft-bristled, large, round brush, firm but not stiff enough to tear tissue, brown paper, iron

FLOWERS: First, you should accumulate a selection of pressed flowers. Wherever you go, look for attractive flowers, grasses, and weeds. Small flowers and leaves that are not very bulky work best. Delicate grassy weeds are often effective, and pansies press beautifully. Lay flowers between pages of an old catalog, or sheets of newspaper, and put something heavy on top to make sure they dry flat. Check frequently and change papers to absorb all moisture. Most flora are ready in about two weeks. Delicate ones take less time to dry.

When you have an assortment of dried materials, sort them and keep them in boxes. (Flat hosiery boxes are good for this.) Then you can choose what you need for each arrangement.

TO ARRANGE: On a piece of white paper, draw an outline of the folded stationery (4″ × 5½″ for the design illustrated). Arrange flowers (and pressed butterfly, if you have one) in this area, experimenting until you get a pleasing composition. Handle the flowers carefully. It may help to use a pencil eraser to move them around as you arrange them.

The shapes of the flowers often suggest their own arrangement. For instance, start with a large flower—a pansy perhaps—placed somewhat low and left of center (Fig. 1). From this, swing up grasses and ferns using the natural curves. Bring a few out to the right at the bottom and add some tiny flowers.

TO ASSEMBLE: The next step is to draw the outline of an opened piece of stationery on white paper (5½" × 8"). Indicate fold with a line (Fig. 2). Cut piece of wax paper about 7½" × 10", and lay it over outline.

You are now ready to assemble. Mix white glue (half water, half glue). Put in shallow dish. With large round brush, dab glue on wax paper in work area to hold flowers in position. Don't worry if the glue beads up. Just be sure there is enough in the needed area. Transfer your flower arrangement to the wax paper, one piece at a time, with background pieces first, then flowers.

Take a single ply of facial tissue and gently lay over entire 7½" × 10" area. With brush, dab more glue solution over tissue without shifting or brushing. Gently dab straight down. Start with flowers and work out toward edge. The surface should be generously dabbed over, but every spot need not be covered. Uncovered areas create a lovely texture (Fig. 3). Area over flowers, however, should be thoroughly saturated with glue. Dab a solid line of glue along edges also. You will have a textured sandwich, wax paper at back, tissue in front, with flower arrangement between.

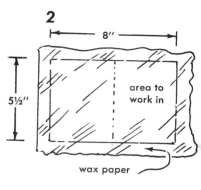

TO FINISH: When glue is dry, press with a warm iron between sheets of brown wrapping paper. Trim to 5½" × 8" (or size needed). Fold in half and slip around the folded stationery sheet. The message will be written on the paper; the flower section can be slipped off and reused or framed.

Once you have the dried material, the glue thinned, and a working place set up, you'll find it easy to make several of these. Three pieces with envelopes make a nice gift or a package to sell at a bazaar.

VARIATIONS

Make small version for gift enclosure.

To frame a piece of Oshibana stationery, slip the decorated flower piece off the stationery, and trim off back. Place arrangement in a purchased frame with colored paper behind flowers.

If you wish to *plan* an Oshibana for framing, make the flower arrangement to fit standard frame with glass, using complete area 8" × 10" (size of the tissue). Follow the steps above. Lay Oshibana over a piece of colored

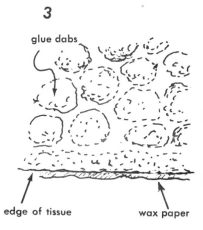

paper, frame, and hang.

Another use for these lovely arrangements is a cosmetic or perfume tray. Purchase an appropriate frame with glass. Using a man-sized tissue (about 11″ square), make the flower arrangement to fit. When Oshibana is finished, place over a piece of colored paper, one that brings out the beauty of the flowers. If necessary to fill frame, cut a mat to fit the frame and to fit over the arrangement. Many frames come with mats already cut. Frame it in the same way as you would frame a picture. Cut a piece of felt large enough to cover back of frame. Glue felt along the edges of frame in back to protect the furniture surface. When dry, trim felt even with edge of frame. Then, instead of hanging it, set it on your dresser or vanity.

GLASS PENDANT

The action of water and sand on shards of broken glass produces a lovely effect, rounding the edges and texturing the surface. Next time you find an irresistible shape on the beach, save it to make a piece of jewelry. A lens from an old pair of sunglasses may be used instead of beach glass. Follow instructions below. See color photograph facing page 136.

MATERIALS NEEDED
Piece of water-washed beach glass about 1½″ × 2″
Small roll of copper wire (from picture-hanging department)
1 tiny shell (or bead or jewel)
Epoxy glue or household cement
Chain (or thong or necklace) for suspending pendant
Also needed: heavy scissors or wire cutters, narrow-nosed pliers, toothpick

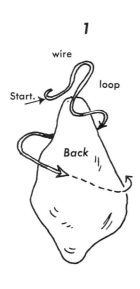

PENDANT: Unwind some copper wire from roll. Make a hanging loop (Fig. 1), using pliers. From top back of glass piece (below loop), wind wire down and around. Hold each turn with fingers as you pull wire around. Try to achieve graceful sweeps of wire to complement natural curves of the glass. Wind three or four times around, each time at a different angle. Fig. 2 suggests one possible method. Finish winding in front. Leave about ¾″ and cut wire. Twist a small end loop in front

(Fig. 3). To complete hanging loop, use small pliers to twist end into a back wire (Fig. 4).

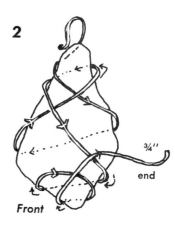

2

Front   ¾″ end

ADD A TINY SHELL at the tip of front wire end. Reshape wire, if necessary, so twist fits neatly around the shell. When satisfied with arrangement of wires around glass, mix some epoxy glue. With a toothpick apply a tiny dab of glue under the shell and on the twisted end of the wire. Glue shell onto wire, and glue wire loop down onto the glass. Add dabs of glue at sides, if necessary, to keep wound wire from slipping. Add glue on top in back to cover wire twist and hold top loop in position.

TO COMPLETE: Hang pendant from leather thong or cord, tying to top loop of pendant (Fig. 5). Or slip chain through top loop (Fig. 6).

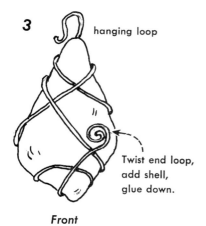

3
hanging loop

Twist end loop, add shell, glue down.

Front

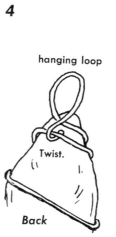

4

hanging loop

Twist.

Back

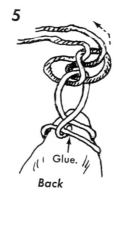

5

Glue.

Back

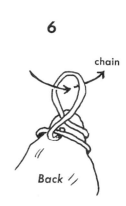

6

chain

Back

VARIATIONS

This copper-wire cage can be used to suspend any natural treasure: a polished piece of agate, a flat shell, a piece of coral.

If you use a lens from an old pair of sunglasses, remove the colored-glass shape from the frame. Wind with copper wire (Fig. 7). Be aware of patterns formed by the crossing of wires in back, since they show through the glass and create delicate traceries. For decoration, add a small gem, a piece of gemstone (from a rock tumbler), a fake jewel, or an ornamental bead. Glue as described above. Hang on chain or thong.

To make a pin from an old lens, cut a small print (from a Christmas card or museum catalog) to size and glue it to inside. Allow to dry. Trim edge and attach pin-back with clear household cement.

7

TISSUE BOX

See color photograph facing page 56.

An inexpensive new box or a dingy old one can be refurbished and personalized. Just choose decorative designs that fit the recipient's life style, and use colors that match her room. Once you have decided which motifs and hues will work, it should be easy to select fabric, yarn, and paints for this purpose.

The simple art of stenciling, used here, can be adapted to many craft projects.

MATERIALS NEEDED
Tissue box, plastic or metal (smooth surface)
10″ × 16″ fabric scrap (approximately)
2 yds. each of bulky yarn (or rug yarn) and regular yarn (contrasting colors)
Acrylic paint (2 or 3 colors)
16″ × 10″ piece backing paper from adhesive-backed vinyl (or sturdy paper or stencil paper from art store)
Scrap paper or newspaper
Lightweight paper
Synthetic kitchen sponge
Also needed: Pencil, black felt marker, pencil knife or single-edged razor blade, saucer or shallow dish, fabric glue, masking tape

PLAN box covering. Select color scheme and motif. Fig. 1 shows a variety of motifs. Choose fabric to cover box. It should be a fairly sturdy, opaque fabric, such as linen or linen-texture synthetic, burlap, or tweed. Color should be light beige, white, or other very pale color so stenciled-on designs will show.

TO MAKE PATTERN: Lay top of box face down on scrap paper and cut size needed (Fig. 2) to cover top and sides. Fold paper around so corners meet, and trim as needed. Allowing a little extra all around, cut this shape from the fabric.

1 MOTIFS

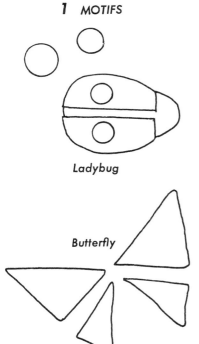

Ladybug

Butterfly

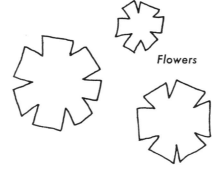

Flowers

Leaves

TO ATTACH TO BOX, smooth a thin layer of fabric glue over top of box. Lay fabric on and smooth down. Add glue to each side, smooth and stretch fabric over the sides. Butt the corners. If there is some overlap at corners and bottom, it can be trimmed later. For a top-opening box, cover top. Measure and fit strip of fabric around sides. Allow glue to dry thoroughly. From inside top of box, cut out oval-shaped opening with sharp scissors or a single-edged razor blade.

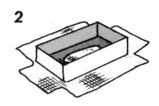

2

ALLOW TO DRY, checking occasionally to make sure fabric has adhered properly all over the box. When dry, trim the hole in top as close to the edge as possible. Trim corners and along bottom edge. Add tiny dabs of glue at the corners, if necessary, to butt firmly and neatly.

3

TO MAKE STENCILS: Trace motif desired on lightweight paper (see Fig. 1). For ladybug, make one tracing of orange areas, another tracing of black area and dots.

Cut backing paper into pieces about 2″ × 3″ (larger for butterfly). Tape design on a piece of the backing paper. (If you use regular paper for stencil, give it a coat of spray-on varnish, front and back, before making stencil.)

With knife or razor blade, cut out shape. Each color needs a separate stencil (Fig. 3).

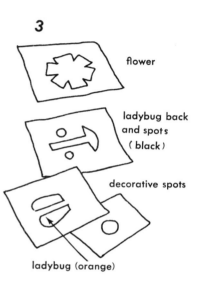

flower

ladybug back
and spots
(black)

decorative spots

ladybug (orange)

TO ADD DESIGN ON BOX: Plan where each element will go. Make interesting groupings; shapes can overlap slightly in a few places. Mark the general placement lightly with a pencil. Tape a stencil in place.

TO PAINT: Squeeze a little paint into the saucer. It is usually about the right consistency directly from the tube. If too thick, thin with water. Wet the sponge (ordinary synthetic kitchen sponge) and wring out thoroughly. Dip a small area of the sponge into the paint. Dab sponge onto some scrap paper to test paint thickness and practice achieving the proper texture (Fig. 4). Paint should be applied in a light layer, allowing some of the background to show through.

Dab sponge over stencil, laying color in the cut-out portion. Some of the texture of the fabric should show through. The paint needs to be just thick enough to show color and stencil outline.

Lift the stencil. Check to be sure there is no paint on the back.

Tape stencil in another position and repeat. Stencil first color and shape in all areas planned.

4

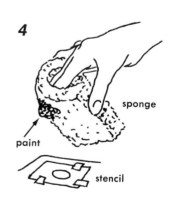

sponge

paint

stencil

Add antennae.

5

Add antennae.

Add body.

See color photograph facing page 56.

Wash dish and sponge. Then wring out sponge. Squeeze another color into a saucer and repeat, using stencil planned for second color. If you wish a third color, repeat, using a third stencil shape. Wash dish and sponge.

TO FINISH: Squeeze a line of fabric glue along bottom edge of box top. Glue on bulky yarn. Glue regular yarn (contrasting color) next to bulky yarn. These hide the cut edge. Have ends meet at a corner. When glue is dry, clip so they will butt. Add a little glue to secure. Repeat, adding yarn on cut edge of fabric around top hole.

For box with lid that opens, glue yarn around edge of lid, and around sides where lid and box meet.

To complete ladybug or butterfly designs, draw in antennae with black felt marker, as needed (Fig. 5). If you prefer, thin black yarn can be glued in curves to suggest antennae.

Should you wish a hard finish, flow on a clear acrylic finish with a large brush. Or spray with a special finish made to cover cloth.

VARIATIONS

Choose any desired motifs with a simple outline. Designs shown in magazines for needlework or painting can be traced. Stenciled initials make the tissue box a very personal gift.

This stencil technique can be used to decorate any object. First, paint the surface or glue on fabric. Then stencil. Match a canister set to curtains, match chair backs to seat covers, etc. Or pick up the design in a sheet and transfer it to bedroom accessories, such as a wastebasket, knickknack box, or a hand mirror. If you plan to stencil loose fabric (such as curtains), stretch it tightly and tack down with thumbtacks before you begin.

Be very neat and precise when stenciling. Acrylic paints will *not* wash out, so make sure paint gets onto fabric *only* in the exact places planned.

RIBBON EYEGLASS CASE

The eyeglass case illustrated is made from wide, decorative ribbon. The felt is used both as background and liner. The ribbon can be as wide as 2¼″ or as narrow as 1″ to be effective. Cover just one side of the case if you have only a 7″ scrap of elegant ribbon. Simple ribbons can be embellished with beading, fake jewels, or other fantasies.

MATERIALS NEEDED

14″ of decorative ribbon, 2″ wide
7″ × 6″ Felt (color harmonious to ribbon)
½″ × 6″ piece of lightweight buckram or other stiffening material
Fabric glue (optional)

CUT FELT AND SEW: With matching thread, make a ⅜″ hem on bottom end as shown (Fig. 1), using a catch stitch (Fig. 2). Fold top hem over ½″ strip of buckram and catch-stitch (Fig. 1).

Fold felt around and butt unsewn edges together. Catch-stitch these edges together. Sew bottom end closed (the end without the buckram), using small, invisible stitches.

SEW ON RIBBON: Fold end of ribbon ½″ down inside top. Using catch stitch over hem (Fig. 3), sew end down. Sew ribbon onto felt around outside of case, using a blind stitch. Make the stitches as neat and invisible as you can. Fold ribbon over when you reach the top. Cut off, allowing ½″ inside. Finish by catch-stitching the end of the ribbon inside the hem. (You can glue ribbon on with fabric glue instead of sewing, if you prefer.)

VARIATIONS

Since only small pieces are needed, all kinds of small scraps and sample swatches of elegant fabrics can be used. Narrow ½″ ribbon alone makes a striking accent for brocade or other fancy fabric.

If using fabric instead of felt for eyeglass case, cut a piece 7¼″ × 6½″. Turn under ⅛″, then make ⅜″ hem top and bottom (Fig. 4), with buckram inside top as before. Fold case around (wrong side out) and stitch a ¼″ seam by machine. Press seam open (Fig. 5). Turn right side out. Finish bottom and add ribbon as before.

If you have a talent for petitpoint or embroidery, you can use a panel of this handiwork instead of ribbon.

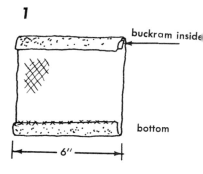

1

buckram inside
bottom
|← 6″ →|

2

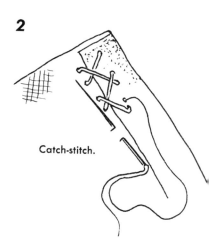
Catch-stitch.

3

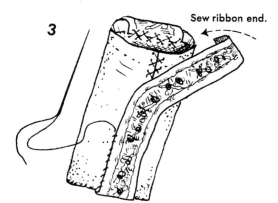
Sew ribbon end.

4

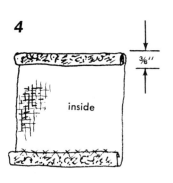
inside
⅜″

5

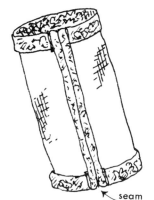
seam

RAINBONNET CASE

The method is exactly the same but simpler. Eliminate the buckram. Cut felt 4″ × 5″, ribbon 9″.

Fold over and sew or glue ¼″ hems (Fig. 6). Continue and finish, using the same procedure as for the eyeglass case. If ribbon is bulky, sew (or glue) on only one side to cover seam.

PINCUSHION

See color photograph facing page 56.

This pincushion is actually a covered styrofoam ball stuck into a base made from an inverted spray-can top. By adding weight as suggested below, you will give it a more luxurious "feel," but neatness and elegance are even more important here.

MATERIALS NEEDED
7″ square of fabric
Styrofoam ball, 3″ diameter
3″ diameter spray-can top (cap), metal or plastic
Weights (drapery, fishing weights, or pebbles)
Four ¼″ beads for "feet" (pony beads, cluster beads, or nail heads
    with prongs turned in)
Epoxy glue, fabric glue
For the Boutique Pincushion on page 58, various trims such as:
    10″ of plastic gold beads
    10″ gold gimp braid
    5 gold foil corners or medallions 1″ high
    3 beads
    Corsage pin
Also needed: Serrated knife, toothpicks, rubber bands

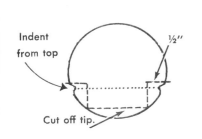

Cross section of whittled ball

TO SHAPE BALL: Push it into cap and twist slightly, forming a ridge as a guideline. With a serrated knife, whittle out the styrofoam, making an indentation about ½″ in and ½″ above ridge and creating the mushroom shape shown (Fig. 1). This indentation allows room for fabric gathers. Cut bottom tip off ball.

TO MAKE A PATTERN FOR COVERING: Draw a circle 6½″ in diam-

Ribbon Eyeglass Case (page 54); Rainbonnet Case (page 56), Apron (page 63); Tote Bag (page 59); Pincushion (page 56); Napkin Ring (page 141); Ladybug Pot Holder (page 61); Tissue Box (page 52)

Grow Chart (page 98); Blob Batik (page 136); Metal
Flower Arrangement (page 20); Owl Collage (page 21)

eter on paper. Then draw five wedges as shown in Fig. 2, which need not be exactly spaced out. Cut wedges out of circle and discard them. Pin circle to fabric and cut out.

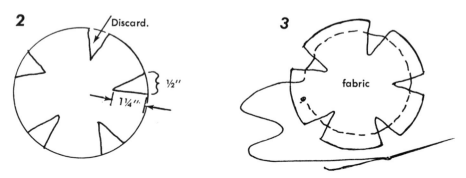

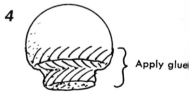

ATTACH FABRIC: Make a running stitch about ½" from edge around circle and across cut-out wedge shapes (Fig. 3). Apply fabric glue on ball in areas shown (Fig. 4). Place fabric around ball and pull up thread like a drawstring (Fig. 5), knotting ends. With a toothpick, add glue under any cut edges and stick them down so they don't show. As glue sets, smooth fabric around ball to allow a minimum of gathers. You will find that knit or stretch fabric adapts most easily to the round contour. Set ball aside.

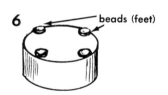

TO PREPARE BASE: Using epoxy glue, stick firmly inside cap anything that is heavy (small hardware, fishing weights, pebbles). Make sure they are securely glued so they won't rattle. Also check space carefully so that the ball has room to fit down inside. Let weights set.

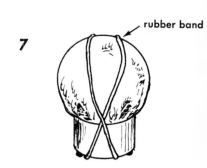

TO FINISH BASE: If can top is a good color, use existing finish; otherwise, spray black or gold or any color that looks well with the fabric. When dry, turn cap over. With epoxy, glue beads to base for feet (Fig. 6). Allow glue to set thoroughly.

TO ASSEMBLE PINCUSHION: Apply fabric glue inside edge of cap, and push covered ball down inside. Hold with rubber bands until dry (Fig. 7).

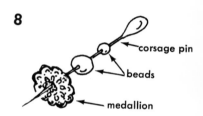

DECORATIONS: Choose an imaginative theme for decorating. Glue trim around where ball joins cap. Add another row of trim at base. If you wish, insert a top ornament. Put corsage pin through beads and medallion (Fig. 8). Add styrofoam glue to pin and push down into ball.

VARIATIONS

With resourcefulness you can create many different "looks." A few are shown here.

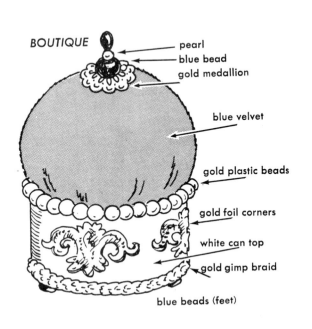

BOUTIQUE

pearl
blue bead
gold medallion
blue velvet
gold plastic beads
gold foil corners
white can top
gold gimp braid
blue beads (feet)

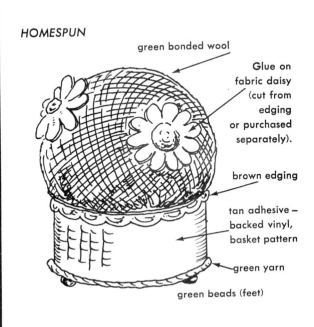

HOMESPUN

green bonded wool
Glue on fabric daisy (cut from edging or purchased separately).
brown edging
tan adhesive— backed vinyl, basket pattern
green yarn
green beads (feet)

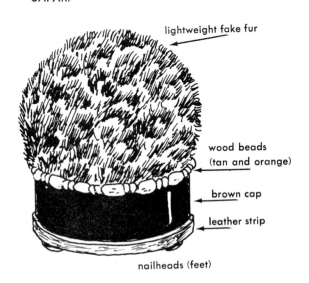

SAFARI

lightweight fake fur
wood beads (tan and orange)
brown cap
leather strip
nailheads (feet)

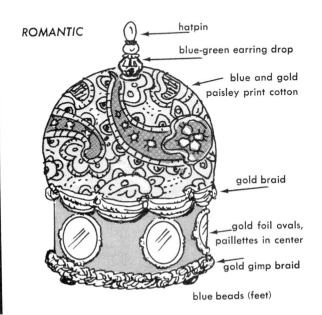

ROMANTIC

hatpin
blue-green earring drop
blue and gold paisley print cotton
gold braid
gold foil ovals, paillettes in center
gold gimp braid
blue beads (feet)

TOTE BAG

Place mats have been used to make the front and back panels of the illustrated tote bag. But any sturdy fabric can be substituted. The side inserts and handle are made of decorative trim.

MATERIALS NEEDED
2 woven fabric place mats, 12″ × 18″, or two pieces of sturdy fabric
    cut to this size (any color)
3 yds. 2½″ wide decorative cotton trim in contrasting color
Also needed: Needle, thread to match trim, pins

SIDE AND FRONT PANEL: Fold over 3″ at one end of the trim and sew. Fold down 3″ of one end of the place mat (Fig. 1). For outside decoration, keep mat's fringe on edge and side of the 3″ top fold-over. Remaining fringe should be sewn inside when attaching trim.

    Using thread to match the trim, start sewing trim and mat together. (Arrow in Fig. 1 points to the upper left-hand corner of front of bag where sewing begins.) Continue down side of place mat, attaching trim to mat with overcast stitch. Try to keep stitches invisible. At bottom, ease a little extra trim to allow for turn of corner (Fig. 2). Remember that the trim forms the sides and bottom of the bag.

    When reaching the top of the 3″ fold on the right-hand corner of the place mat, allow an extra 3″ of trim before cutting off. Fold the three inches inside. Turn end under and sew down (Fig. 3).

*See color photograph
facing page 56.*

1

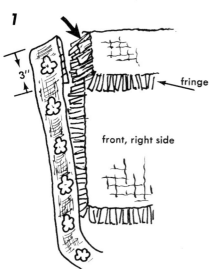

2

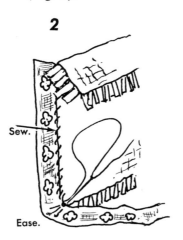

3

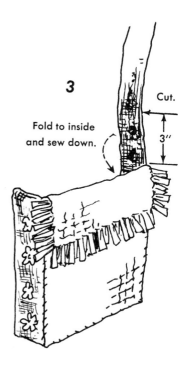

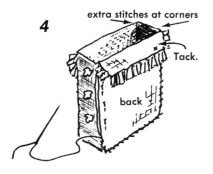

4

extra stitches at corners

Tack.

back

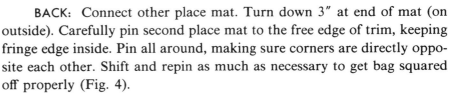

BACK: Connect other place mat. Turn down 3″ at end of mat (on outside). Carefully pin second place mat to the free edge of trim, keeping fringe edge inside. Pin all around, making sure corners are directly opposite each other. Shift and repin as much as necessary to get bag squared off properly (Fig. 4).

Starting at top of back mat, attach trim as before. At four top corners, sew over a few extra times to reinforce. Sew a few small stitches near fringe, tacking down the decorative fold-over.

HANDLE: Use remaining piece of cotton trim. Fold over 16″ and sew the two thicknesses together (Fig. 5).

Pin other end of trim (single thickness) to front of bag as shown (Fig. 6) above fringe. Pin trim down front (centering on bag), across bottom and up the back. Sew neatly and firmly. Bring handle (double thickness) around, and fold in outside corners of end of trim to form a wide V shape. Overlap trim in front. Sew down with tip about 3″ below top edge (Fig. 7). Then stitch along both edges of V and up each side of handle to top of bag. Sew inside of handle firmly to top of bag.

VARIATIONS

If you make the tote bag out of a sturdy fabric instead of mats, turn the 3″ top fold inside so that the wrong side of the material doesn't show. Trim the edges of the fold slightly so fold-over will fit inside without wrinkling (Fig. 8). Turn under edges of fold-over ¼″ and stitch invisibly to inside of front. Do the same to the back piece before attaching trim. Proceed as above, allowing ½″ of fabric all around for seams.

For economy's sake you may wish to substitute contrasting fabric for the decorative trim. Cut strips of fabric 3″ wide. Turn under edges ¼″ and sew by machine on each side of strip. Then attach to mats (or fabric) as before.

If your hobby is weaving, hand-woven panels make magnificent tote bags.

5

16″

Sew to front.

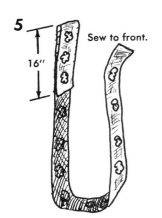

6

front

handle

7

Sew.

top front

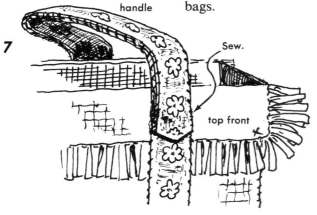

8

fabric inside

Trim off.

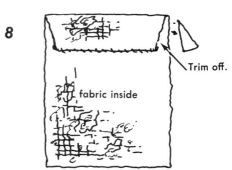

LADYBUG POT HOLDER

Terry cloth, which comes in a wide range of designs and colors, is one of the most practical materials for pot holders.

For padding, used material is equally sensible since it shaves the cost, and pot holders should be inexpensive. Edges of worn-out terry towels can be used. Ironing-board padding is excellent too, for it often has a heat-reflector surface. And here again, the edges are often usable after the center has gone. Of course, all used material should be thoroughly clean and fresh.

To make a special gift, try a shaped pot holder like the terry cloth ladybug described below.

See color photograph facing page 56.

MATERIALS NEEDED
8½″ square of orange terry cloth (for more elegant texture, use a washcloth of velour terry—or a towel, to make several)
8½″ square orange cotton fabric (or black)
8½″ square used material for padding (see above)
4″ square black felt (or small scraps), or black cotton (but allow ⅛″ extra to turn under when you appliqué pieces)
5″ black middy braid or cord
1 yd. black bias binding

ENLARGE PATTERN on paper following outside line for orange shape. Make another paper pattern for black head and dots.

TO CUT: Place body pattern on fold of orange terry fabric. Cut out. Make same shapes for cotton lining and for padding. Cut out black felt head, laying pattern on fold of fabric. Cut six black dots.

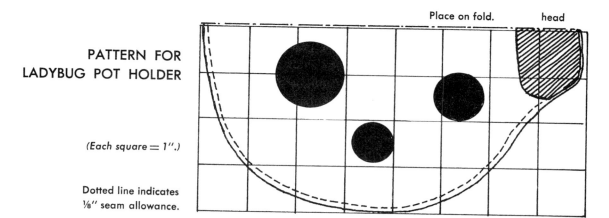

PATTERN FOR
LADYBUG POT HOLDER

Place on fold.   head

(Each square = 1″.)

Dotted line indicates
⅛″ seam allowance.

If you wish to get two pot holders from one washcloth (Fig. 1), make one of the pot holders in two pieces. Stitch a ¼″ seam along the center back spine, and allow for this when cutting. Sew up seam before continuing.

TO ASSEMBLE: Lay three pieces together, padding in the middle, terry on top (right side out), orange cotton beneath (right side out). Pin along center fold. Machine-stitch along fold line with piece laid flat. Fold down along stitching, letting under-layers of fabric stick out somewhat (Fig. 2). With pot holder folded, smooth fabric and carefully pin the three layers together all around edge. Allow the under surfaces to protrude as far as necessary. Baste together, making sure you do not pin or sew to other half of pot holder.

Open and stitch along edge of the terry (as basted) about ⅛″ from the edge all around. Trim off the padding and lining materials that protrude, so they are even with the terry.

TO FINISH: Cut 8″ piece of bias binding. With shape opened flat, hand-sew binding along back spine over machine stitching. Sew rest of binding around the edge, to cover stitching and raw edges all around. Appliqué head and black dots in position, according to the pattern.

HANGING CORD: Fold black cord in half. Place ¼″ inside top of head at spine. Pinch head together and sew around cord and sew edges together about ⅜″ down from spine. This shapes the head (Fig. 3) as it attaches the cord. Sew other end the same way. This preserves the fold-over shape.

VARIATIONS

Flat pot holders are merely two 6″ squares with padding between. To make these, fasten the three layers together neatly with bias binding, adding a loop at one corner. (Check a purchased holder for construction.) Choose a decorative terry with designs adaptable to pot holder-sized squares. Many pot holders can be cut from a single patterned towel. Use this for one side, with plain terry cloth or cotton fabric for the underside.

1

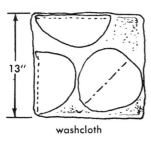

washcloth

2

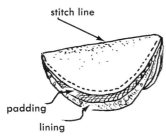

stitch line

padding

lining

3

Sew.

Sew ⅜″.

padding

bias binding

APRONS

Aprons make excellent gifts, since they offer such variety of styles, from the cocktail frivolity to simple, all-purpose coverall, and everything between. The half-apron described below is made of practical plastic.

MATERIALS NEEDED

2/3 yd. (orange) plastic runner (sold for protecting rugs) usually about 27" wide

1 yd. (orange and brown) cotton fringe, 2" wide

60" striped 1" wide grosgrain ribbon (yellow, brown, and orange)

Also needed: Pins

See color photograph facing page 56.

PLASTIC RUNNERS are available in many grades and types. Some are too lightweight and tend to wrinkle and tear. The heavier weights may have molded-in studs, not practical for an apron. Best to use is a medium weight which often comes in lovely crystal colors. The one shown is orange with textured stripes.

CUT PLASTIC 18" × 27". For pocket, cut piece of plastic 5½" × 6" with stripes going across. For pocket decoration, cut a 6" piece of fringe.

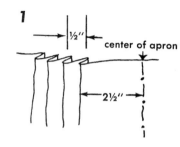

PIN four ½" pleats on each side of top of apron in position shown (Fig. 1). Baste in position and remove pins. This should gather the top to about 19". Because plastic is a little bulky, measurements and pleating cannot be too exact. Just try it on and see if it is a comfortable apron size.

WAISTBAND: Center ribbon on top and pin to plastic, leaving about 20" of ribbon at either side for sash ties. Top of ribbon band should be 1/16" above edge of plastic. Using a long machine stitch, sew ribbon to plastic ⅛" from edge of ribbon, top and bottom. Make a double row of stitching at corners where tie sash begins (Fig. 2).

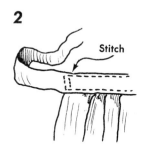

POCKET: Fold down ½" of top edge of pocket piece. Machine-stitch across twice, ¼" apart (Fig. 3). To make flower-shape decoration, curve the 6" piece of fringe into a circle, making motifs meet. Then place fringe circle on pocket, pin, and sew around by hand at the point where stitching

4

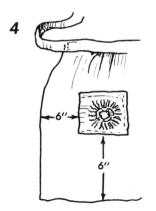

already exists. Sew down through plastic, allowing fringe to spread out like a flower.

PLACE POCKET on apron in position shown (Fig. 4). Pin in center to hold that position. Attach with double row of stitching, the outside row ⅛″ in from edge of pocket, the other row ¼″ inside of this (Fig. 5). At top corners, to make a neat square of stitching, lift presser foot, turn apron, lower presser foot, and continue. Square corners also help reinforce top of pocket.

BOTTOM DECORATION: Sew remaining fringe by hand to lower edge of apron. Allow ½″ extra each side. Plastic should be about 1″ down behind fringe so only loose part of fringe hangs below plastic. Width of stitched area of the fringe will determine how far up on the plastic you should place it. Make two rows, and follow stitching that already exists in fringe. Fold back extra pieces on ends and sew behind.

5

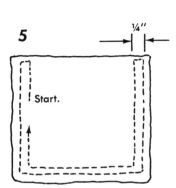

VARIATIONS
Most half-aprons are merely a piece of fabric gathered into a waistband. Cut fabric 21″ long and 34″ wide. Make small side hem and 3″ hem at bottom. Gather top to 17″ and sew on waistband of fabric or ribbon, allowing ⅜″ seam. Cut pocket to allow ⅜″ fold under. This is an average size, but aprons should vary in size to meet various needs.

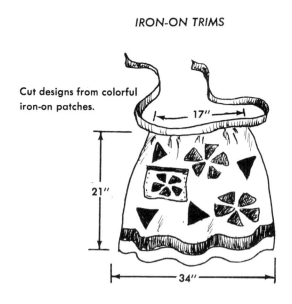

IRON-ON TRIMS

Cut designs from colorful iron-on patches.

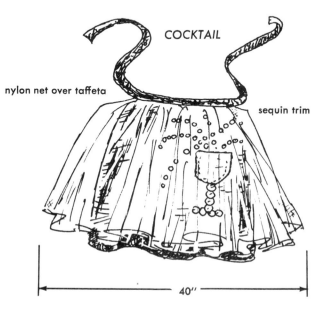

COCKTAIL

nylon net over taffeta

sequin trim

Look for unusual materials among household fabrics, as well as dress fabrics. Patterned bath towels can be converted into aprons, and end-of-season sales may yield a colorful beach towel large enough for several aprons. If you use terry cloth, you can add matching hand towels or pot holders (attach at waist with Velcro®).

Be sure to include pockets on all aprons. Keep the apron trim simple if you are using a "busy" fabric. For coverall and bibbed aprons, it is best to work from a purchased pattern.

You can decorate aprons in many ways. Here are a few suggestions for half-aprons:

BOLDLY GEOMETRIC

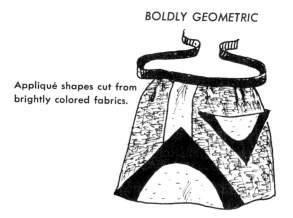

Appliqué shapes cut from brightly colored fabrics.

CHILD'S APRON

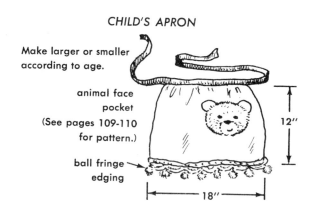

Make larger or smaller according to age.

animal face pocket (See pages 109-110 for pattern.)

ball fringe edging

12"

18"

FOR CHRISTMAS

red waistband

green corduroy

Appliqué a dancing Santa.

(See pages 44-45 for pattern and instructions.)

PATCHWORK

Use up odd pieces. Or appliqué pieces over a solid background.

(See page 80 for planning patchwork.)

4. GIFTS THAT WILL PLEASE MEN

Making gifts for the men and boys in your life can be a challenge, but the ones that succeed often become sentimental treasures. For those you love —father, husband, brother, or son—selecting and making presents should be fairly easy. Who knows better their needs and tastes? When using a picture as part of your project, choose a subject allied to the recipient's hobby or special interest and thus stamp the gift with his own personality.

For other men in your life, less intimately known, a handmade remembrance is often the best solution for gift-giving. These one-of-a-kind presents will be well appreciated by bosses, partners, clients, or friends on any occasion. Certain projects outlined in Chapter 2, "Decorative Gifts for the Home," can be adapted for office use when you don't wish to give too personal a present. The secret of success is in choosing colors and textures.

In creating practical items for men and boys, try to appeal to their particular interests, select suitable materials, and keep your workmanship neat and precise.

EMBOSSED HERALDIC BOOKMARK

Embossing is simple to do and, in this case, makes good use of discarded material. The bookmark offers a good project for practice. Once you have learned the technique of embossing, you can progress to other pieces, adapting other decorative motifs. Glue embossed panels to boxes, desk accessories, bookends, and wastebaskets to produce attractive gifts for anyone—particularly men.

MATERIALS NEEDED

1 disposable aluminum container (from TV dinner, cake, or large pie)

½ yd. narrow soutache braid (red)

8½" × 1¾" piece blue felt

Small piece of absorbent cotton

Walnut stain

Fabric glue

Also needed: Old scissors, several thicknesses of newspaper, dried up ball-point pen, wooden stick (from ice cream, craft-stick), masking or cellophane tape, brush (for stain)

TO MAKE PATTERN: Trace heraldic design (Fig. 1) on paper. If you want to make a more personal gift, you can replace one section of the design with initials (as in Fig. 2).

FOR ALUMINUM STRIP, cut out the bottom of the pan with an old pair of scissors. From this bottom piece, cut strip measuring 7" × 1¼". With the rounded wooden stick, smooth out any design or embossed printing that is on the cut-out strip.

TO MAKE EMBOSSING: Place tracing of design on the aluminum piece. Tape in place. Copy outline of design with the ball-point pen. Remove pattern. Turn aluminum strip over. Lay face down on padding of several thicknesses of newspaper. With the ball-point pen, gently work the outside edge of the shields, and stripes on the shields, until these outlines are indented. Work the same way on lines defining other elements.

Now, working within these outlines, go over each area (shaded in Fig. 1) several times, using a scribble motion in the stripes. Go over line of

aluminum strip

red soutache

flat areas (unshaded)

embossed areas (shaded)

blue felt →

PATTERN FOR HERALDIC BOOKMARK

(actual size)

1

2

stars until they stand out on front side.

As you work, turn piece to front side to see how embossing has progressed. With stick, smooth flat areas around the design on the front side. This will help to raise the embossed areas. Work until the design stands out clearly.

TO KEEP EMBOSSED AREAS RAISED: Turn strip to back side, apply glue behind the shields and wide stripes, and stick in little dabs of absorbent cotton to fill indentations. Let dry.

TO COLOR: Brush strip with walnut furniture stain on front side. Let stand a few minutes, then wipe off gently, leaving some color in the recessed areas. Dry overnight. Polish lightly with a soft cloth so raised areas will shine.

TO ATTACH BRAID: Apply a thin line of glue around outside edge of piece on front. Starting at one corner, attach red soutache braid over glued edge. Wipe off excess glue with a damp cloth.

TO ATTACH BACKING: Glue aluminum strip in position on the blue felt strip (8½″ × 1¾″).

See color photograph facing page 96.

EMBOSSED EAGLE BOX

The never-ending uses for boxes always make them welcome gifts for a man.

MATERIALS NEEDED
Wooden box, approximately 5½″ × 4″ × 2″ (new from a craft supply, an empty cigar box, or any old box, sanded and cleaned)
Paint: white latex, black latex (or enamel or spray), spray silver, varnish
Foil pie plate
1 package ½″ sequin pins
Absorbent cotton
²/₃ yd. silver gift-wrap cord
5¼″ × 3¾″ red felt (or cut to fit easily inside cover of box)
5½″ × 4″ black felt (or size of base of box)

Also needed: Masking tape, ice-cream stick, dried-up ball-point pen, fabric glue, small hammer, screwdriver, old newspapers (for padding), old scissors

TO PREPARE BOX: Paint with white latex inside and out. Spray inside of box silver. When dry, paint outside black. Glue silver cord around top edge. Finish box with several coats of dull-finish varnish.

EAGLE: Trace pattern (below) on paper. Cut out flat part of foil pie plate. Tape eagle pattern to the foil. Trace design on foil through paper with dry ball-point pen. Remove paper. Emboss the design (see page 67). Working from the back, use pen to shape chest, head, and center of feathers. They should appear raised in the front. A rounded wooden implement, such as an ice-cream stick, is also helpful in making the larger raised areas, such as the chest. On front, press down between feathers, press in line for eye, etc. Cut eagle out of the foil, around edge of shape. Emboss more if needed.

TO RETAIN EMBOSSING: Saturate some cotton with glue, turn eagle over, and place tufts of cotton on the back. This should be done in areas that are most raised on the front, such as chest, large feathers, etc. These areas need padding to avoid flattening down if something is set on top of the box.

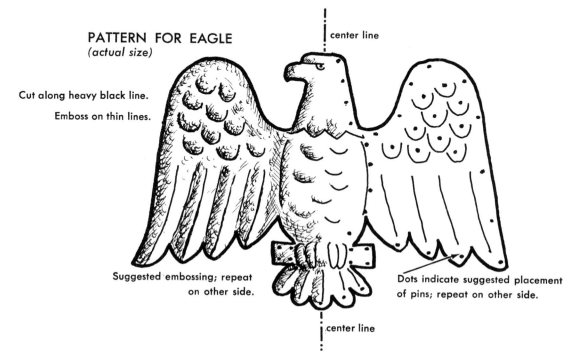

PATTERN FOR EAGLE
(actual size)

center line

Cut along heavy black line.

Emboss on thin lines.

Suggested embossing; repeat on other side.

Dots indicate suggested placement of pins; repeat on other side.

center line

TO ATTACH EAGLE TO BOX: After glue-saturated cotton is dry, place two sequin pins at either side of chest. Tap in gently with a small hammer, being careful not to flatten the embossing. These pins should keep the eagle from slipping. Place the remaining pins on the wings in the center of each top feather and on tip of each long feather (see pattern). Put one pin in for the eye. Add pins at tip of each tail feather.

Ends of pins may come through inside cover. Fold these over and flatten with tip of screwdriver.

Using pen, go around edge of foil (without denting wood of box), turning edges of foil under slightly. Also reshape any embossing that was lost during insertion of pins.

TO FINISH: Glue red felt inside top of cover to hide pin ends. Glue black felt to bottom of box.

VARIATIONS

Other interesting items can be glued to the top of a box, such as a montage of playing cards, postage stamps, etc. Whatever you choose, make a pleasing arrangement. Add appropriate cord trim.

DECOUPAGE

Boxes may be decorated by gluing a print to the cover, then varnishing. (This is a simplified version of découpage.)

Use any box (preferably wood), old or new. Select a color to complement the print, and use it to paint or stain the box. Glue print on top (see bookends, page 71). If possible, find appropriate pictures to fit the sides also. If not, cut small spots out of a larger print and glue them to the sides. Or glue on decorative trim. Add cord or trim to edges. Cover with a light coat of spray varnish. When dry, antique lightly with walnut stain if you wish. Finish decorated box with several coats of brush-on varnish, or cover both print and trim with shellac. Let varnish or shellac dry thoroughly before adding another coat.

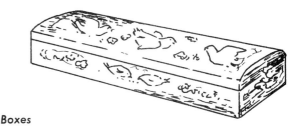

Boxes

BOOKENDS

A small investment of time will produce a quality gift appealing to book lovers.

See color photograph facing page 96.

MATERIALS NEEDED
1 pair plain wooden bookends with simple metal bases (available at department stores, or through mail-order houses)
Old maps, prints, or other suitable pictures
1 yd. gold paper edging about ¼″ wide
1 yd. narrow gold rickrack (plain or adhesive-backed)
White glue
Clear varnish, matte finish
Also needed: Brush (for varnish), damp cloth, pushpins or thumbtacks, fine sandpaper, single-edged razor blade

PREPARE BOOKEND: Sand wooden surface lightly. On tracing paper, make outline of the shape. Use this to help you select the proper size scene or picture you need for decorating the bookends.

SELECT PRINT: The pictures do not need to be identical, but they should be similar in color, subject, and scale. On the bookends illustrated, small sections of old map prints were used. Old greeting cards and museum catalogues are good sources. Choose reproductions of paintings, nature studies, sports scenes, or whatever you feel will enhance this gift for the particular man receiving it.

When you find a pair of scenes that fit within the outline, trace outline on each print. Cut out, about ⅛″ larger than needed.

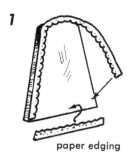

1

paper edging

TO ATTACH: Turn print over and apply white glue. (Thin with a little water if too sticky to spread evenly.) Centering print, glue to wooden bookend. Press down and smooth out bubbles. There will be a slight protrusion around the edges. When dry, the print can be carefully trimmed to make it flush with the edge of the wood.

TO DECORATE FRONT: Starting at base, apply a thin line of glue on edge of print and apply paper edging up and around, curving to fit (Fig. 1). Glue a straight piece across the bottom. Dab off any excess glue with a damp cloth.

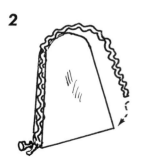

TO DECORATE SIDES: Stick on adhesive-backed rickrack around edge. Or apply a line of glue around cut-edge thickness of wood. With a pushpin or thumbtack, fasten plain rickrack at bottom corner. Stretching rickrack slightly, glue up and around and tack down to other corner at base (Fig. 2). Press smooth and remove excess glue with a damp cloth. When dry, remove tacks and cut rickrack even with bottom.

TO FINISH: Using a clean brush, add several coats of clear matte varnish or plastic finish to bookends, covering rickrack and trim. Insert base into upright (Fig. 3).

VARIATIONS

Some craft-supply stores carry unfinished wooden bookends (Fig. 4). The side that will not be covered with a picture would need painting or staining before the project is started. Such bookends are often ¾″ thick, so a wider edging or double rows of rickrack would be needed for the sides (Fig. 5).

Wooden bookends can also be decorated with wood-burning. Select a simple motif, outline with wood-burning tool, or texture edges with tool, gluing picture in center (Fig. 6). Finish as before.

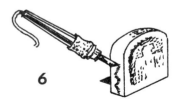

WASTEBASKET WITH "SCRIMSHAW" PANEL

This wastebasket offers a rich combination of textures that belies its homely beginnings. No one would guess that the elegant decorative panel is merely a section of a bleach bottle. It has the rich look of old etched ivory. Many years ago, sailors on whaling ships occupied their idle time by etching whale's teeth. Their handiwork was called scrimshaw, and some of it can still be seen in museums today.

You can also use this kind of decoration on smaller containers for various uses.

MATERIALS NEEDED

Small metal wastebasket (about 10″ high)

1 yd. adhesive-backed burlap

2½ yds. brown or black edging or decorative edging in color to complement burlap

5½″ × 9″ piece of opaque white plastic (cut from a gallon bleach bottle)

Brown furniture stain (dark maple or teakwood, or brown paste-type shoe polish)

Fabric glue

Contact glue or heavy grip cement (inquire at hardware store for best product to attach plastic to metal)

Also needed: Masking tape, carbon paper, paper for pattern, heavy darning needle, soft cloth rag, weight, tape measure, brush for stain

See color photograph facing page 96.

COVER WASTEBASKET with adhesive-backed burlap. If basket has straight sides, use a tape measure to determine size of covering. Cut out, allowing a little extra. If sides of basket are sloped, tape newspaper around basket to make a pattern. Trim paper to fit. Lay paper pattern on backing of burlap, trace around and cut out. Peel off backing and stick burlap to basket. Trim off any extra.

TO MAKE DECORATIVE PANEL OF IMITATION SCRIMSHAW: The 5½″ × 9″ piece of bleach bottle is used for this. Later, piece will be trimmed to 5″ × 8¾″, but you will need a little extra now to hold onto while working. Use only the part of the bleach bottle that has no ridges or glue spots. Flatten by rolling piece in opposite direction of curve. Tape down.

On a piece of paper, draw area and plan your design. Choose a traditional subject, such as an old sailing ship, or a contemporary motif, such as butterflies or mushrooms. Use greeting cards or magazine pictures as guides. Trace or copy freehand. Don't worry if the drawing is crude. The old sailors who made scrimshaw had no artistic training. It is the primitive quality that gives scrimshaw its charm.

Tape pattern onto plastic piece. Lay carbon paper between. With a pencil, go over drawn lines of design to transfer it to the plastic.

Remove carbon and paper. With a heavy darning needle or opened safety pin or sharp compass point, scratch into the plastic surface, outlining design and adding details. Short scratches make waves, dark areas can be filled in with criss-crossed scratches (Fig. 1). The decoration can be as elaborate or as simple as you want it to be. Areas with considerable scratching will appear darkest in finished design.

When scratching is completed, cover surface of plastic with brown wood stain (or brown paste shoe polish). Let stand a few minutes. (Time varies with different brands of stains, but don't let it dry.) Gently wipe off stain with a soft cloth. The surface will be a mellow tan color. The dark brown color of the stain will be retained in the scratched areas revealing the design. The color does not have to be wiped off evenly; variations of color enhance the effect. If you wipe off too much, put on more stain and repeat until the desired brownish-ivory color is achieved. Allow to dry.

TO ASSEMBLE: Trim scrimshaw down to 5″ × 8¾″. Place panel on covered wastebasket. Determine best location and trace around panel. Using utility knife or single-edged razor blade, cut panel area out of the burlap covering. Peel off. Glue scrimshaw panel to basket, following instructions on glue container. Lay basket on side, put a box or books inside for support, and place a weight on panel until glue sets.

TO COMPLETE: Using fabric glue, attach edging around panel and around base and top of basket.

VARIATIONS

Instead of covering with adhesive-backed burlap, materials such as fake leather, burlap, vinyl, denim, or vinyl-wallpaper leftovers can be used. Attach with fabric glue. This basic idea can be adapted to make many things such as these desk accessories:

PENCIL HOLDER

Use a soup can with top neatly removed. Clean the can and spray-paint inside if desired. Cover, trimming off just below top ridge. Make a panel of scrimshaw 3″ × 3″, or make it go all around the can (Fig. 2), if you want it to look more like a piece of ivory tusk. In this case, add fabric above and below panel. Glue edging top and bottom. Glue a cork circle down inside to fit the bottom of the can, and a felt base underneath.

BOX

Stain or paint a box, make a panel to fit top, and glue on cord edge around panel.

LETTER BASKET

Use an empty gallon can (a container for such products as floor wax, turpentine, or cooking oil). With tin snips, cut off top of can (Fig 3). Discard top half. (Wear heavy gloves until the cut edges are completely covered, since the cut areas can be quite sharp!) Draw a line 4″ from base. With tin snips, trim down neatly along this line. Clean can thoroughly. Spray-paint base,and inside of can.

    Glue a piece of twine or cord around top edge (Fig 4). Cut covering material 21½″ × 5″. Attach to can, overlapping slightly in back. Allow 1″ to stand up above top of can. Cut a slit on each corner down to can edge (Fig. 5). Neatly fold the burlap (or other material) down inside, over the top edge of the can. Press down firmly all around over twine and down inside. Make a scrimshaw piece, then trim to about 4½″ × 2¾″. Cut burlap or other material out of this area on front. Glue panel to can. Glue edgings around panel and base. If desired, cut a piece of felt or cork to fit inside base (Fig. 6). Add a dab of glue and insert inside letter basket. Glue felt under bottom of can.

3

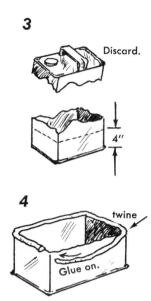

4

5

6

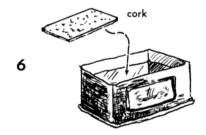

GLASS PAPERWEIGHT

A scene in miniature, under a glass dome, makes an interesting paperweight. Minute figurines are usually found in gift departments, but a variety of little plastic animals can be purchased in toy stores. Once encased in glass, they will look almost as elegant as expensive ones. Scenery and figures made for miniature railroads are also effective. Keep your eyes open, for suitable material appears in the most unexpected places.

    In buying the glass for this paperweight, select one that makes an attractive, clear dome when inverted.

MATERIALS NEEDED

Juice or cocktail glass (as round shape as possible) about 2½″ across
   rim
3″ metal jar top
Self-hardening clay or homemade clay (page 33), tinted green if
   desired
Assorted tiny objects (The one shown contains tiny pine cone, china
   duck, scrap of driftwood, plastic flowers less than ½″ diameter.)
12″ decorative cord
12″ flat edging, ⅜″ or ½″ wide (depending on rim of jar top)
Small fishing or drapery weights
3″ circle of felt
Epoxy glue, fabric glue

TO MAKE BASE: Fill jar top with clay (Fig. 1). To provide necessary mass for the paperweight, insert fishing leads or drapery weights into the clay. Shape the clay smooth, slightly below the edge of cover. In the paperweight shown here (Fig. 2), a piece of driftwood was pushed into clay near the center, a small figurine placed in front, pine cone and tiny plastic flowers arranged around. Place the pieces where you want them. Set glass dome over them frequently to make sure it fits and that the arrangement looks attractive through the glass.

   After determining the arrangement, remove figurine and plastic flowers, clean, and set aside. (Glue in position later.)

   After clay is thoroughly hard (follow instructions for type of clay used), complete arrangement. Glue pieces in place.

   TO ATTACH GLASS TO BASE: Glue rim of glass to the clay with epoxy.

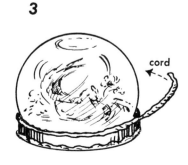

   TO FINISH: Add cord around rim where it is attached to base (Fig. 3), using fabric glue. This cord makes the joining more secure and more attractive.

   Glue fabric or paper edging around jar-top rim, completely covering it. A wide ½″ ribbon can be used, or possibly two rows of middy braid would cover this area.

   TO PROTECT FURNITURE SURFACES: Attach felt circle under base, using fabric glue.

VARIATIONS

Less expensive than a glass would be a small baby-food, pimiento or similar round jar. Just be sure that you use a base slightly larger than the mouth of the jar.

HARDWARE PAPERWEIGHT

Unusual hardware will make an interesting and successful paperweight. Search or ask for large, heavy pieces, not more than 4″ long. These may be rescued from scrap heaps, or spotted among factory discards. But don't overlook your local hardware store for fairly heavy odd pieces, such as the 4″ bolt used in the paperweight shown here.

See color photograph facing page 96.

MATERIALS NEEDED

4″ bolt
1″ nut
3 screw eyes, various sizes
5″ silver chain (from a cheap bracelet or from hardware store)
Scrap of driftwood (or 3″ × 4″ piece of wood, ½″ thick)
Dark stain (optional)
Epoxy putty
Fabric glue
Silver (aluminum color) spray paint
3″ × 4″ piece black felt (or size needed to fit under base)
Also needed: Pliers (to open chain)

PREPARE METAL AND BASE: If the metal is old and corroded, clean it thoroughly and dry. Spray silver. New metal is attractive without added finish. Select a base of appropriate size for the hardware you have chosen. The illustrated paperweight is mounted on a slab of driftwood (with knothole) cut to 3″ × 4″. If you use plain wood, stain it.

ATTACH hardware (bolt and nut) to base with epoxy putty. Screw in the three screw eyes (Fig. 1). Open link in one end of the chain and put through screw eye on other side of bolt and over to screw eye in corner.

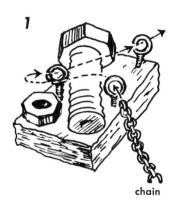

chain

Remove as many links as necessary to make it tight. Put link around screw eye and close. Then rotate last screw eye until chain is taut. The chain doesn't really hold anything; it is just decorative.

See color photograph facing page 96.

FINISH by gluing felt to base with fabric glue. Then paperweight can be used safely on a desk.

HARDWARE PENCIL HOLDER

For a companion piece to the paperweight, make a pencil holder out of hardware.

MATERIALS NEEDED
Piece of metal pipe, 4″ high, 2″ inside diameter
3½″ square of wood
Silver (aluminum-color) spray paint
Black paint (or stain)
17″ piece of silver-color chain (from hardware store)
2″ circle of cork (or art foam)
3½″ square of felt
Epoxy putty, household cement, or clear epoxy glue
Also needed: Sandpaper, pliers (to open chain), pencil

1

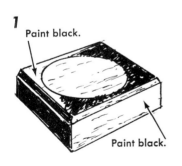

Paint black.

Paint black.

CUT WOODEN BASE, bevel edges slightly with sandpaper. Set pipe on base and draw around it, making circle on the wood. Paint base black ouside of drawn circle (Fig. 1), or stain. Spray pipe with silver.

TO ATTACH: Mix epoxy putty according to directions. Put a line of putty around bottom edge of pipe and press pipe onto the base. (Putty adheres best to unpainted surfaces.) Clean away any excess.

2   link

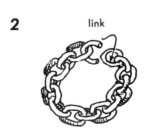

TO TRIM: Measure chain to fit around pipe. Open links to get proper length. Reclose link around end, forming a circle the right size for the pipe (Fig. 2). Slip over pipe and slide down to the bottom. This chain will hide any putty that shows. Dab on some household cement where links hit bottom of pipe. Add another circle of chain at the top. Glue a small section at a time with household cement or clear epoxy glue. Hold until set, repeat, and continue around.

TO FINISH: Trim cork circle to fit inside pipe. Add dab of glue underneath cork, insert in pipe and push down in with a pencil until it is firm against bottom. With fabric glue, add black felt under base. Trim even with edge of wood.

PATCHWORK BAR-B-QUE APRON

See color photograph facing page 96.

This apron is a great conversation piece, as well as a cover-up for the man who cooks out-of-doors. Each ornamental brand is decipherable, though guessing what each one means may take a few trys. If you give the apron as a gift or make it for a bazaar, tuck in a note decoding the brands. (See brands on pages 81 and 82.)

MATERIALS NEEDED

¾ yd. colored denim (or other sturdy fabric 36″ wide or more)

Nine 10″ × 10″ (approximately) pieces of similar weight fabric in various harmonious colors

1 package 3¼″ × 7″ iron-on tapes or patches (lightweight) in various colors

1 package bias binding (single fold)

2 curtain rings 1″ diameter

Also needed: Small scissors, pinking shears, tape measure or ruler, pins, pencil or felt marker, newspaper, masking tape

ENLARGE PATTERNS (on page 81) to sizes indicated.

BIB: Pin pattern on fold of fabric (the large piece of denim). Cut out bib.

TIES: Cut two pieces of fabric 5″ wide and 22″ long. For neck loop, cut a piece 5″ wide, 33″ long. (This can be a different color if desired.)

BRANDS: Lay brand pattern on a piece of iron-on tape. Choose a color that contrasts with the patch it will be used on. Then, with small sharp scissors, cut out the brand. Repeat with other brands, using various colors.

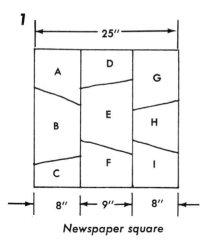

1

25″

A
D
G
B
E
H
C
F
I

8″ ← 9″ → 8″

Newspaper square

BOTTOM SECTION OF APRON: Make a patchwork of shapes to suit the scraps of fabric you may have available. Three of the patches should be at least 7″ × 8½″ to feature the brands (A, E, and G in Fig. 1).

TO MAKE A PATTERN FOR PATCHES that will fit neatly together, cut a piece of newspaper 25″ square. (Tape extra piece on one side to make it large enough.) Decide on shapes of the patchwork areas you want to make and draw them with a felt marker on this square of paper. For instance, shown here (Fig. 1) are three panels composed of three patches each, cut at interesting angles. Label paper patches with letters (or numbers), so you will know position of each when sewing. Cut the paper along the lines you have drawn. The edges of these pieces represent the *stitching* lines. To get the cutting edges, lay each of these pieces on another piece of newspaper. Draw around edge of a paper piece, then draw a ½″ margin all around (Fig. 2). Repeat on all pieces. Label each piece and cut out of the paper.

Pin pattern A on the fabric selected. (Choose scraps to make an interesting arrangement of colors.) Cut out of fabric. Repeat for other pieces.

TO SEW PATCHED SECTION: Stitch all patches together by machine with ½″ seams. Sew bottom of A to top of B; bottom of B to top of C. Repeat with other two strips. With pinking shears, pink seams and press open. Then sew the three strips together. Pink seams just sewn and press open.

TO ATTACH BIB: Sew it to top of patchwork squares. Finish edges of bib and bottom section of apron by machine or hand, sewing bias binding to side edges, right sides together (Fig. 3). Then fold binding around to back and sew down by hand (Fig. 4). Make 1½″ hems across the top of the bib and across the bottom of the apron.

TIES AND NECK LOOP: Fold pieces in half lengthwise and stitch a ¼″ seam. Continue stitching across one end (Fig. 5). Turn all three pieces right side out and press flat.

2

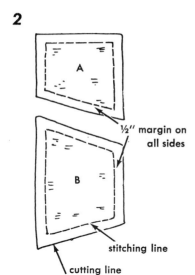

A

½″ margin on all sides

B

stitching line

cutting line

3

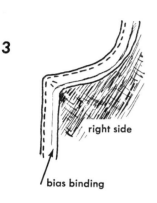

right side

bias binding

4

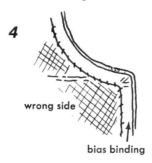

wrong side

bias binding

5

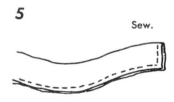

Sew.

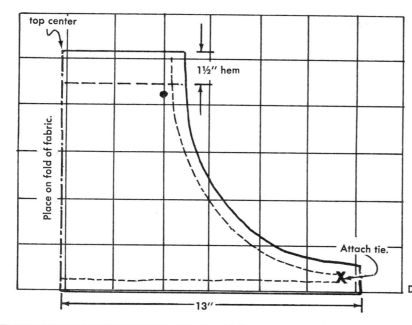

**PATTERN FOR
BIB OF APRON**

(Each square = 2".)

top center

1½" hem

Place on fold of fabric.

Attach tie.

X

Dotted lines indicate ½" seam allowance.

13"

PATTERNS FOR BRANDS

(Each square = 1".)

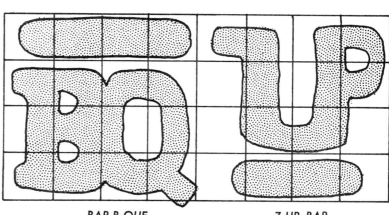

BAR-B-QUE   7-UP BAR

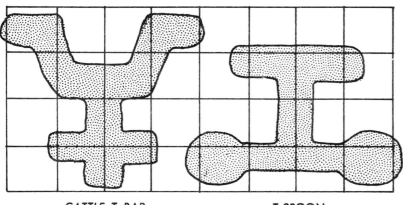

CATTLE T BAR   T-SPOON

Pin the finished end of tie below lower corner of bib and sew tie into position by machine-stitching along bound edge. Cut end of tie at angle, fold raw edges inside, and sew together (Fig. 6). Repeat on other side.

Sew finished end of neck loop piece inside left top corner of bib. Finish other end, using same method as for ties. On right top corner of bib (right side of material), sew two curtain rings (Fig. 7). To use, pull neck strip through both rings and tuck back through one ring. This makes neck loop adjustable.

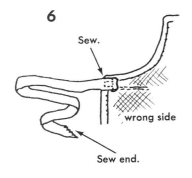

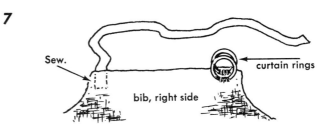

TO APPLY BRANDS TO CLOTH: Use a dry iron, following instructions on the package of tape. Place the "Bar-B-Que" brand in the center of the bib section. Place the other three brands in patches A, E, G (or arrange differently).

Press entire apron.

VARIATIONS

Below are suggestions for additional brands if you wish to substitute them for those given. Possibly you can design a brand with initials to make the apron a more personal gift.

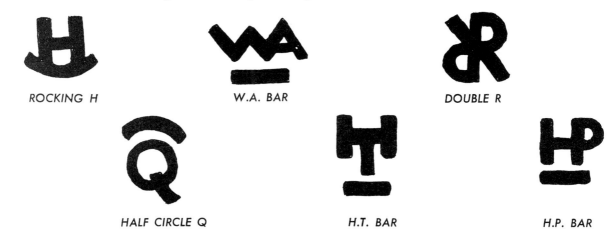

ROCKING H   W.A. BAR   DOUBLE R

HALF CIRCLE Q   H.T. BAR   H.P. BAR

SCENT SENTINEL

When hung in a closet, this sentinel removes dampness and odors without adding any fragrance of its own.

See color photograph facing page 96.

MATERIALS NEEDED

4″ × 6″ felt (or bonded fabric) for front
4″ × 6″ firmly woven cotton for back
Iron-on tapes: 1½″ × 3″ pink, 1½″ × 3″ black or navy, ½″ × 2″ red.
5 paper fasteners, ½″ long
12″ chenille pipe cleaner
2/3 yd. gold middy braid, 2″ loop braid
Black felt marker
Crumbled clay granules (sold in pet shops and supermarkets for use in cats' boxes), about 2/3 cup
3″ × 4″ lightweight cardboard (for tag)
Fabric glue

TO CUT THE POINTED HAT: Pin the two pieces of fabric together. Cut off corners, as shown (Fig. 1). Unpin.

TO DECORATE FRONT: Trace shapes in Fig. 2. For hat brim, cut a 3″ strip of navy iron-on fabric. Fold and cut curve ½″ wide at center, tapering out to ends, following pattern. Cut two pieces of navy iron-on tape ¾″ × ½″ for feet, a strip ¼″ × 1½″ to make division between legs. Fold red piece in half, and using pattern, cut red mustache; open. Iron on the pink piece for face. Iron on all other pieces in position, using drawing as guide for placement. Make eyes with black felt marker.

TO ASSEMBLE: Place right sides of fabric pieces together, pin, and stitch by machine, making ¼″ seam all around edges, leaving bottom open. Turn right side out.

HANGING LOOP: Use chenille pipe cleaner. Fold in half, inserting ends of pipe cleaner into top point of hat between stitches. To hold shape of hat, push in pipe cleaner so ends come out at both corners (Fig. 3). Pull ends out about ¼″ and fold over to front. Twist pipe cleaner at top, sew around point of hat and outside corners to secure.

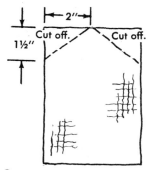

1

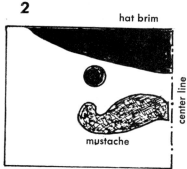

2

Face (actual size)

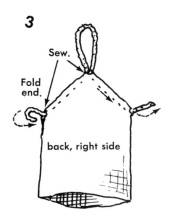

3

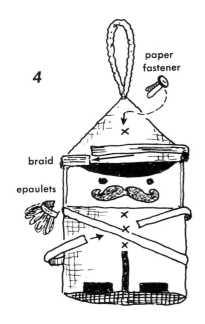

4

paper fastener

braid

epaulets

GLUE gold middy braid around hat, hiding ends of pipe cleaner. Glue braid across chest, around back, ending up again across chest. Push a paper fastener through crossing point on chest to hold and hide ends of braid (Fig. 4). Push in other paper fasteners for decorations (at points marked X on Fig. 4) on hat and chest. Open each in back of felt fabric. Press smooth.

EPAULETS: Cut two 1″ pieces of gold loop braid. With fabric glue, attach at corners on side below face.

FILL WITH GRANULES. Brands vary in consistency. If there is any fine dust, place granules in some scrap fabric and sift out dust first. This will prevent dust from sifting through later. Fill bag and sew bottom of sentinel tightly closed. (If after long use the granules lose their effectiveness, open this seam to refill.)

ATTACH TAG to gift. Letter this note on cardboard.

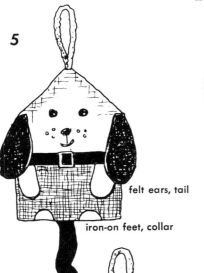

5

felt ears, tail

iron-on feet, collar

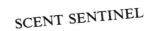

SCENT SENTINEL

A SPECIAL INGREDIENT IN THIS SENTINEL REMOVES DAMPNESS AND ODORS FROM THE AIR. PLACE IN A CLOSET. IT PURIFIES WITHOUT PERFUMING.

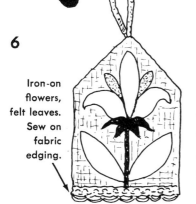

6

Iron-on flowers, felt leaves. Sew on fabric edging.

VARIATIONS

This could also be a child's gift, very effective in a boy's closet. Make a clown or animal shape if preferred (Fig. 5). For a woman's gift, decorate fabric with flower shape or other appropriate designs (Fig. 6).

5. GIFTS FOR MOPPETS

A small child's world lies at his fingertips. In making gifts for him, you should appeal to all the senses, especially touch. So let your presents be bright and colorful, using pleasant and contrasting textures. To these, add sound if you can do so *safely*—a tinkle at least.

Any plaything you create for a child should also be safe for chewing or sucking. Use nontoxic paints (many are so labeled these days), or food coloring when feasible. Make sure edges are well rounded and smoothly finished. Soft plastics, durable vinyls, and foams are most practical materials for the nursery.

Some of the gifts described here for little people can be appealing decorations for a baby's room. They also provide wonderful ideas for a baby shower or things you can give a new mother.

A few of the projects are simple ones, easy enough for a busy mother to make. Others, while easy to assemble, are more time-consuming, so a loving grandmother or aunt can create a very special gift for a favorite grandchild, niece, or nephew. Such an offering is frequently cherished as an heirloom.

KITTEN-LESSON WALL HANGING

See color photograph following page 96.

This may seem to be a decorative wall hanging for a child's room; actually it is a useful teaching toy. If you take it down from the wall, the child can work with it on a table or on the floor. The mittens can be pulled off and easily replaced by just laying them against the kitten's hands! As deftness increases, the child can unzip the bag, tuck all the mittens inside, and zip it closed. The dress can be removed from the kitten on the left by untying the bow. Other jackets unbuckle, unbutton, and unsnap. Also let the child dress the kittens, "find" their mittens, and put them in place. Mittens serve as a test for matching colors, too. Here is something that will keep tiny hands busy while teaching basic skills. When not in use, it should be rehung.

MATERIALS NEEDED

26″ × 27″ piece heavy cotton (duck or sailcloth) or upholstery fabric for background (yellow). Or buy ¾ yd. and cut to 26″ × 27″

Felt: *for kittens:* 9″ × 12″ each; pink, brown, black

    for jackets: 5″ × 7″ each; yellow, green, orange

    for mittens: 3″ × 4″ each; purple, tan, blue

    for eyes: 1½″ × 4½″ light green

6″ × 8″ sturdy fabric for bag (blue)

5″ strips of Velcro® (can be purchased in notion departments; strips adhere to each other)

2 large snaps (sew-on or hammer-on)

Two ⅞″ diameter buttons

2 eyelets (package from notions department comes with directions) or use two ½″ bone rings

¾″ buckle (from old belt) or tab made for kilts (from notion department) or inexpensive wide watchband (optional)

5″ plastic broom bristles (9 pieces) (optional)

1 package 1½″ × 5″ iron-on fabric, various colors (6 pieces)

6″ (or 4″) zipper (blue)

24″ shoelace, white or bright color

Embroidery floss (optional)

30″ café-curtain rod

Also needed: Needle, thread, large needle, fabric glue, felt marker (optional)

Buckle and snap.

VELCRO®

Button on.

Tie a bow.

Zip a bag.

Specific colors for this wall hanging are suggested, but any color combination can be used. Whenever possible, use scraps or sample pieces that are available. Many of the notions may be lying around in your own (or a friend's) sewing box.

TO PREPARE BACKGROUND: Sew ½″ hem on each side of background fabric. Make a 1¼″ hem top and bottom.

ENLARGE PATTERNS (page 88), and make separate patterns for eyes and nose.

CUT two kitten shapes of different colors. Reverse pattern and cut third kitten. Cut two jackets in colors to contrast with colors of kittens at center and right. Cut dress, using dress pattern, for kitten on left. Cut three pairs of mittens of felt, each set a different color. Cut mitten bag of fabric (blue); one piece 2″ × 7½″, other piece 3″ × 7½″.

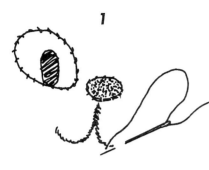

FACES: Cut six eyes of green felt, three noses of scraps of pink or black felt. Sew or glue eyes in place, according to pattern. Using embroidery floss, make an outline stitch for curved mouth on each kitten (Fig. 1). Embroider a black line in each eye. If you prefer, you can draw in lines with black felt marker instead of embroidering.

WHISKERS (optional): Make holes in cheeks with large needle (see dots in pattern), and slide in broom bristles, three for each kitten. Cut a 1″ square of felt or other scrap fabric. Glue on back of kitten, behind nose, to hold whiskers in place.

PATTERN FOR KITTEN-LESSON WALL HANGING

(Each square = 1½″.)

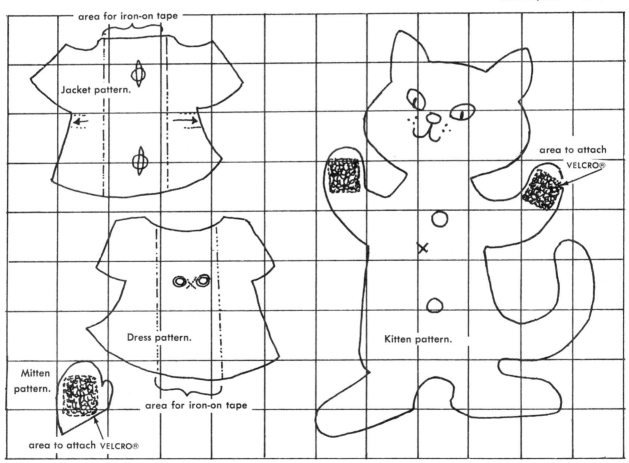

area for iron-on tape

Jacket pattern.

area to attach VELCRO®

Dress pattern.

Kitten pattern.

Mitten pattern.

area for iron-on tape

area to attach VELCRO®

TO ATTACH MITTENS TO HANDS: Cut a ¾″ piece of the fluffy side of Velcro® and sew onto hands in positon indicated on pattern. Cut a ¾″ piece of the other side of Velcro® and sew to mittens in pairs as indicated, flopping mate to each mitten. The Velcro®, which adheres to itself on contact, holds mittens on hands. After the mittens are pulled off, they can be attached again by just placing the two strips of the Velcro® together.

JACKETS AND DRESS: Choose color of iron-on trim to contrast with jacket color. Iron on in position shown in pattern. For re-enforcement, iron on another strip on back of jacket directly behind front strip. Repeat on other jacket and dress.

TO ASSEMBLE: Lay kittens on background and arrange as shown in picture. Pin in place. Sew kittens to background.

KITTEN ON THE RIGHT: Sew the two buttons on kitten at the spots marked with circles in the pattern for the kitten. Sew through both felt and backing. Cut buttonholes in jacket, centering on circles on jacket pattern, and making a 1″ opening to fit over button. Check with buttons already sewn on to make sure buttonholes fit. Cut slits about $^1/_{16}″$ wide (Fig. 2). Button on jacket.

MIDDLE KITTEN: Sew on snaps, or use the hammer-on type of snap fasteners. Place at spots marked with circles on pattern for the jacket. Put snaps on jacket in corresponding position. Snap jacket in position. If desired, add a belt. Cut old belt to make a piece 4½″ long when buckled (or use wide watchband or kilt tab). Place over jacket at spot indicated by arrows on jacket pattern. Sew ends to backing fabric. Make sure jacket is removable when buckle is opened.

KITTEN ON THE LEFT: Make two eyelet holes indicated by circles on dress pattern, following directions on package of eyelets. If preferred, cut out ¼″ circles. Sew bone rings in position for laces (Fig. 3). Sew middle of shoelace in spot on kitten at "X," so shoelace can be laced through eyelets and tied to hold the dress in place.

MITTEN BAG: Turn under and baste ¼″ on all edges of both pieces. With zipper closed, sew zipper, by machine, between two pieces (Fig. 4). Zipper should show. Place piece with zipper on the background fabric

2

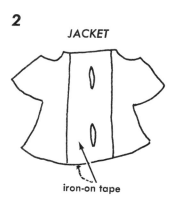

JACKET

iron-on tape

3

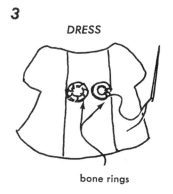

DRESS

bone rings

4

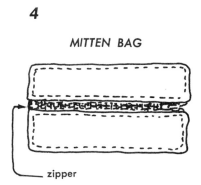

MITTEN BAG

zipper

between the kittens, 2½″ up from the bottom edge. Baste down around outside edges. Stitch around outside edges by machine, and remove bastings. Press hanging smooth where necessary.

TO HANG: Slip café-curtain rod through top hem. Use rod fixtures or picture hooks for placing on wall as a decoration. The hanging should be taken down, and the rod removed, when the child wants to play with the kittens.

See color photograph
following page 96.

LOVABLE BLOCKS

These blocks are square enough to be stacked, yet cuddly soft. Knocking them over won't hurt a thing.

MATERIALS NEEDED
(*for 1 ABC block and 1 picture block*)
Vinyl fabric: the kind used for table covering, ¼ yd. (or small pieces)
     in plain, primary colors plus ¼ yd. in a nursery print design.
     (The edges of used vinyl tablecloths can also be used.)
Yarn, various colors, or scraps of felt
12″ × 18″ foam rubber, 1″ thick (buy it by the foot)
Package of double-fold bias binding (color to contrast with print
     design)
Fabric glue (optional)
Also needed: Yarn needle, pencil, tracing (transparent) paper

ABC BLOCK

CUT six 3½″ vinyl-cloth squares in various primary colors. Cut three pieces of foam rubber 3″ square.

PENCIL a letter on each of three of the vinyl squares (A,B,C). Using thick yarn, embroider letters with simple outline stitch (Fig. 1). Or cut letters of felt and glue on.

TO ASSEMBLE: Sew four of the vinyl squares together by machine, seams to the outside. Allow ¼″ seams (Fig. 2). Pin fifth square to bottom and sew on. Stitch on three sides of last square on top (Fig. 3). Slip the

1

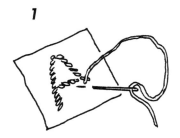

three foam squares inside through opening, one at a time. They should fit firmly and give the block its shape. Pin top down. Stitch remaining edge together by machine, closely as possible, to complete block shape. Compress foam as much as necessary to stitch. Trim seams to ⅛" and trim corners neatly. Sew corners by hand wherever necessary.

PICTURE BLOCK

MAKE the same way, except larger, and use nursery-print vinyl.

2

FOR CUTTING GUIDE: Draw a 4" square on tracing paper. Add ¼" all around for the seam. Lay this paper pattern over design and shift around until you find parts of the design that fit well into that 4" area. Cut out five of these shapes, 4½" square. Also cut one plain-color 4½" vinyl square. Cut four pieces of foam, 4" square.

SEW up vinyl squares as before, slipping foam squares inside to assemble block.

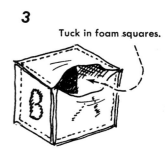

3

Tuck in foam squares.

TO FINISH: Sew bias binding by hand along the seams. Sew to one side of seam, then fold over and sew down on other side. Cover four corner seams (Fig. 4), then sew binding around top and bottom squares. Fold binding slightly to turn corners. Turn ends under to finish (Fig. 5). Binding makes a frame for each block picture.

Gift blocks should be made in sets. If you plan to make several sets, do all the cutting at one time. For variety, blocks can be designed in other dimensions and materials.

4

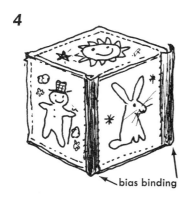

bias binding

5

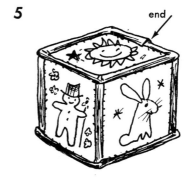

end

JINGLE CATERPILLAR PULL TOY

Noise-making pull toys delight young children. Here's a whimsical jingle-bell caterpillar that is easy to make and easy to love.

See color photograph following page 96.

MATERIALS NEEDED

A 3″ diameter plastic ball (the hollow kind with holes) and three 3″ styrofoam balls

A child's stretch knee sock (medium size, to fit sizes 6 to 8), any bright caterpillar color

3 jingle bells, large size

4 rubber washers, 1″ outside diameter

½ yd. flat or oval elastic, white

6″ baby rickrack

Rubber ring (teething ring, jar ring, or pet-shop ring)

Two 1″ circles white felt and two ½″ circles black felt.

Also needed: Serrated knife, white styrofoam glue, large-hole yarn needle

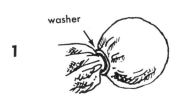

TO PREPARE BALLS: Cut styrofoam balls in half with a serrated kitchen knife. Scoop out a space in the center big enough for a jingle bell to dance around. Put a bell in each ball and glue halves back together with styrofoam glue.

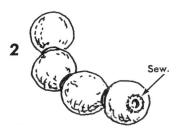

TO ASSEMBLE CATERPILLAR: For head, push plastic ball firmly down into the toe of the sock, stretching it around the ball. Add a washer (Fig. 1). Push in a styrofoam ball followed by another washer. Continue the process, filling the sock. The stretch stock should be just the right size. Pull the top end of the sock through the last washer. Fold back around washer and sew to sock (Fig. 2).

PULL CORD: Thread elastic through yarn needle. Sew through front holes in the "head" (Fig. 3). Tie ends.

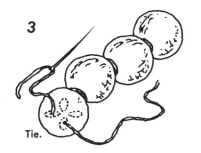

EYES: Sew one black circle to one white circle, and sew the eye in position on caterpillar. Repeat for other eye.

MOUTH: Sew or glue baby rickrack in a curved shape, working around the pull cord (Fig. 4). (Toe seam of sock may guide your curve.)

TO FINISH: Tie a rubber ring to the end of the elastic as a handle for the happy child who receives this gift.

THREE BEARS TOY BASKET

Picking up toys might be a more pleasant chore with the help of a decorated basket.

MATERIALS NEEDED
(for toy basket)
Round plastic laundry basket
Two contrasting vinyl fabrics, ¼ yd. each, usually 54″ wide (sold for tablecloths, etc.)

(for bear decorations)
9″ × 12″ pink felt (two pieces), 3″ × 6″ green felt
Deep pink embroidery floss
9″ white seam binding
1½″ × 3½″ thin white fabric (for apron)
8″ yellow yarn, ½ yd. pink yarn
Three ⅝″ "bone" rings, 1 bead about ⅛″ diameter (optional)
Brown and black felt marker pens
Stuffing (cotton or synthetic)
Also needed: Fabric glue, pinking shears (optional)

TOY BASKET: Determine width of strips to be woven by measuring height of holes in the plastic basket. Cut strips full width of the fabric. Cut enough strips to weave entire basket with alternating colors. Start with bottom row. Weave a strip all around, going in and out of the plastic ribs

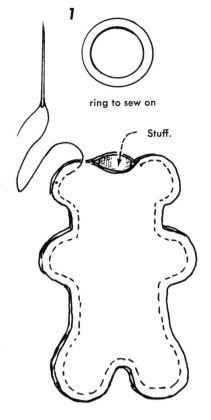

1

ring to sew on

Stuff.

of the basket. When done, woven strip will overlap. Trim off ends of strip so there is about ¼″ overlap. Slide strip slightly so overlap is in back of one of the plastic ribs. Weave next strip above, around the basket, repeating until all rows are woven and ends trimmed. To secure ends, add fabric glue where ends overlap on each row. For decoration, tie on the three little bears.

BEARS: Trace the half-patterns (on opposite page) onto folded paper. Cut shapes of paper and open up for complete pattern of each bear. Enlarge the half-pattern of vest, then draw on folded paper. Cut and open pattern.

CUT two pieces of pink felt for each of the bears. Cut the vest of green felt.

TO ASSEMBLE: Pin baby-bear pieces together. With embroidery floss, sew around bear, using a fine running stitch, about ⅛″ from edge. Leave top of head open and don't cut off thread yet (Fig. 1). Repeat for mamma and papa bears, your outside sewing to measure about $^{3}/_{16}$″ in from edge.

FACES: Color in snout with brown-felt marker. Draw eyes and nose with black marker on each bear.

STUFF bears, then sew top closed. Sew a "bone" ring at top of each.

APRON FOR MAMMA BEAR: Use the piece of white fabric. Pink along bottom edge, if you wish. Fold binding in half lengthwise, sew (or glue) fabric inside as shown (Fig. 2). Tie around mamma bear's waist.

2

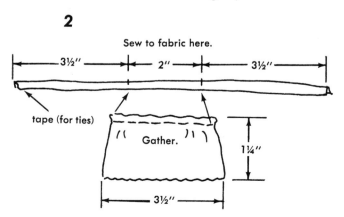

Sew to fabric here.

3½″   2″   3½″

tape (for ties)

Gather.

1¼″

3½″

3

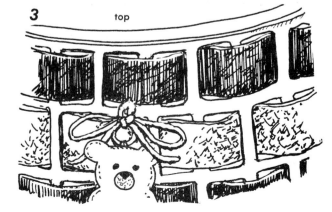

top

shoulder seams ¼"

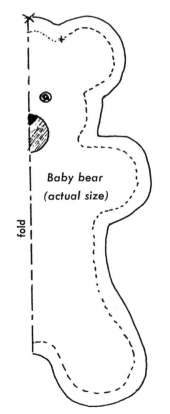

Vest for papa bear
(Each square = 1".)

PATTERNS FOR THREE BEARS

Sew ring here.

Dotted lines indicate
³⁄₁₆" seam allowance.

Dotted lines indicate
⅛" seam allowance.

nose

snout

Baby bear
(actual size)

Mama bear
(actual size)

Papa bear (actual size)

fold

fold

fold

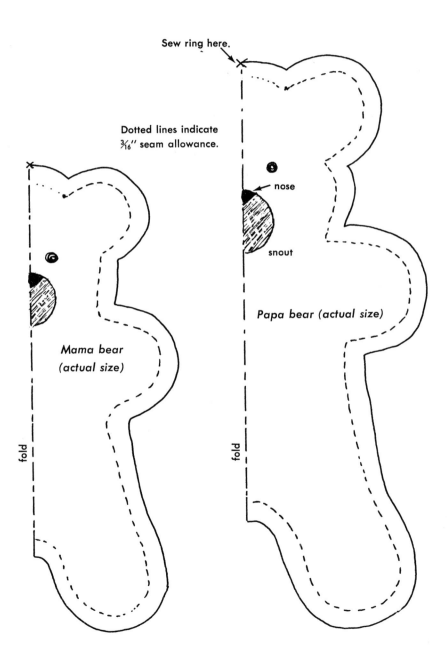

4

PAPA'S VEST: Sew shoulder seams closed overlapping ¼″ seam. Fit the vest around the papa bear. Sew closed at "X." If desired, firmly sew on a small bead at this spot to look like a button.

BABY BEAR: Tie yellow yarn bow around his neck.

TO ATTACH BEARS TO BASKET: Cut three pieces of pink yarn 9″ each. Slip yarn around plastic rib of basket, first row down (Fig. 3), through ring in head of a bear. Tie a bow. Repeat with other bears, spacing them around the basket.

VARIATION:
The bears can also be made for a crib or carriage toy. Cut hanging yarn various lengths. Tie one end of the yarn to the ring in each bear's head, then braid the three yarn ends to make a cord above the bears. Tie end of cord to a larger ring for hanging (Fig. 4).

MOBILE

The motion of a mobile is often one of the first visual stimulations a baby enjoys. Mobiles add charm and color to a nursery and continue to amuse as the child grows. Here is one to start you on mobile-making.

MATERIALS NEEDED
6 plastic practice golf balls (the hollow kind with holes large enough
    to insert straws)
Box of large, round, colored plastic drinking straws
6″ diameter embroidery hoop (one piece)
Fishing line, thin, transparent
Epoxy glue (or glue made especially for plastics)
White enamel paint and brush cleaner (optional)
Small paint brush
Also needed: Toothpicks, crochet hook

*See color photograph
following page 96.*

Wastebasket with "Scrimshaw" Panel (page 72); Patchwork Bar-B-Que Apron (page 79); Hardware Pencil Holder (page 78); Bookends (page 71); Embossed Eagle Box (page 68); Scent Sentinel (page 83); Hardware Paperweight (page 77)

Jolly Jingle Bird Puppet (page 121); "Whufo"—A Beanbag (page 113); Grenadier
Ring Toss (page 114); Elephant Pajama Bag (page 117); Drum Bank (page 112)

PAINT embroidery hoop white. Allow to dry. (Hoop can be left natural color if you prefer.)

TO DECORATE BALLS: Use two matching color straws to each ball. Cut straws in half. Pieces should be approximately 4″ long. Poke straws through the holes in the ball (Fig. 1), making ends stick out in as many directions as possible. Put straws in five of the balls. Cut four 12″ pieces of fishing line. Using a crochet hook, pull line through two top holes of four of the balls and tie. Cut a 20″ line, and tie to fifth ball for hanging in center.

The straws generally fit into the holes and stay in position, but to make sure they won't slip, glue in place. Mix some epoxy glue. With a toothpick, place a small dab around the hole where each straw has been inserted. Shift straw slightly to force glue in. Put dab of glue on knot of line at top of ball.

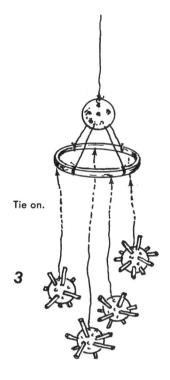

3 Tie on.

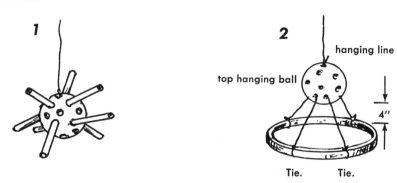

1

2

hanging line

top hanging ball

4″

Tie.   Tie.

TO ASSEMBLE TOP OF MOBILE: Tie four 10″ lines to sixth ball (the top hanging ball). Tie these lines out to the embroidery hoop, leaving about 4″ between ball and hoop (Fig. 2). Space lines approximately equidistant around hoop. Tie 18″ (or as much as desired) of line to top for hanging line.

TO ADD OTHER HANGING BALLS: Attach four straw-studded balls between each line that is tied on the hoop, then pull up to make lines various lengths, such as: 3″, 3¾″, 5″, 6″ (Fig. 3). Hang to check balance. When satisfied with arrangement and balance, dab epoxy (or household cement) on each knot around hoop and top ball. Allow to dry. Trim off all excess ends of lines.

Tie remaining ball in center to top hanging ball (Fig. 4), allowing it to hang down about 13″. Glue knots and trim ends.

This is a basic mobile construction.

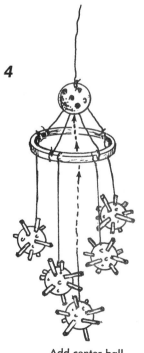

4

Add center ball.

VARIATIONS

Insert flower picks (used in artificial flower arrangements) and glue in holes of the plastic balls for a posy mobile. Or insert colorful plastic toothpicks in styrofoam balls.

To make a natural color mobile for a den, stick wooden toothpicks in cork fishing bobs, and hang from wooden embroidery hoop. Or hang various colorful bicycle reflectors to make a mobile that catches the light.

All sorts of shapes can be hung; for example, small plastic toys or just simple colorful circles. Glue foil gift-wrap to cardboard, then cut out circles. Your imagination will suggest other interesting materials for this purpose.

GROW CHART

A grow chart is an unusual, colorful addition to any child's room. This one also serves as a family tree. It could be an inspired gift project to surprise the family when a new baby arrives.

On page 103 is an instruction sheet that should be duplicated and given with the grow chart so that recipients will know how to use it.

MATERIALS NEEDED

2 yds. yellow sailcloth (or any sturdy fabric, such as poplin, denim, etc.) cut 21½" wide

¼ yd. brown slipcover fabric (54" wide)

Felt: 9" × 12" piece each of light, medium, dark green, medium pink, deep pink, lavender, and blue; 5" square of orange

2 plastic tape measures (lines marking inches should go completely across)

Bulky yarn sold for hairbows, or package ties (assorted colors), 6 pieces cut 14" long

Decorative edging of yarn flowers about 1" wide (optional)

6 buttons, medium blue (preferably flat with 4 holes) 1¼" diameter

Sheet of gold punch-out numbers (from stationery or variety store)

2" narrow white elastic

Cardboard, lightweight (cut 6 circles, 3" in diameter)

Also needed: Fabric glue (optional), small gold safety pin, chalk, small plastic bag, café rod (optional), felt marker

See color photograph
facing page 57.

ENLARGE PATTERNS on page 102 as directed. For flower, fold and trace other half. Cut out all shapes in the colors indicated. Cut six flowers of various-color felt.

For tree trunk, measure an area 5″ × 49″ on the brown fabric with chalk or pencil. Draw a line from center point on top to outside corners at bottom, forming a very tall triangle (Fig. 1). Add ¼″ all around to be turned under. Cut out. Cut branches of the same brown fabric, following patterns.

TO PREPARE BACKGROUND: Cut yellow background fabric 67″ × 21½″. Fold under ¼″ along each side as you make a 1″ hem. Pin, then stitch. On top and bottom, fold under ¼″ and make a 3½″ hem. As you sew across, leave 3½″ open in center of bottom hem. Sew firmly at each side to create a pocket in the back (Fig. 2).

MEASURES: Hand-sew tape measure on each side, leaving 3″ of the tape hanging below bottom of fabric (Fig. 3). Each tape measure should be about ½″ from outside edge. Sew ends of hem closed. Fold the hanging 3″ of each tape measure so that it rests against the back of the hem. Sew on two small pieces of elastic to hold ends of the tapes in place. This not only allows the grow chart to be hung 3″ off the floor, but also will give a more accurate measurement of the child's height.

TREE: Turn under edges of trunk and branches ¼″ and baste. Pin trunk in place on yellow fabric along center line. Lay on branches and space properly up the trunk, using the diagram on page 100 as a guide. When you are satisfied that the branches are the right height and angle, tuck ends under the trunk and pin. Sew on tree by hand (or by machine, using a zigzag stitch).

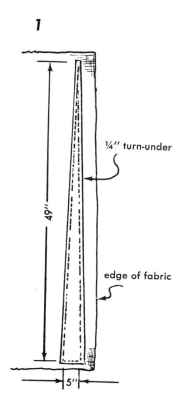

1

¼″ turn-under

49″

edge of fabric

5″

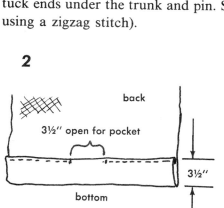

2

back

3½″ open for pocket

bottom

3½″

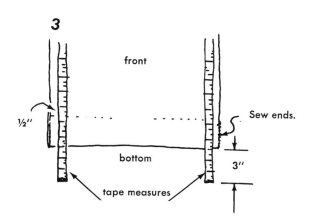

3

front

½″

bottom

tape measures

Sew ends.

3″

tape measures

6

5

4

3

2

1

blue

purple

pinks

brown

DIAGRAM OF GROW CHART

This drawing is in scale. If you have difficulty placing the units, you can make a full scale pattern. Draw 1" squares on paper, and lay it over this drawing. Trace off the design. Then tape several pieces of paper together and draw on 6" squares to enlarge the pattern.

However, it should be possible to assemble the tree without making the huge pattern, just for placement.

FLOWERS: Position large flowers at ends of branches, with tip of branch going just under the edge of the flower. Sew down along the dotted line around the circle as shown in pattern. Position leaves, scattering them about the tree. Sew or glue on.

BIRDS: Sew on (or glue) one bird, and reverse felt for the other bird (to fly in opposite direction), as shown in diagram. With felt marker, draw eye on each (or embroider if preferred).

4

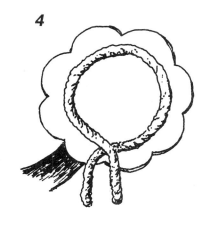

BASE: Pin light green base piece in place and sew down. Then pin and sew dark green piece, overlapping light green base. For small flowers, cut apart the floral edging and scatter flowers around base. Pin and adjust arrangement. Sew or glue on. (Or cut some ¾" diameter felt flowers, and sew or glue on.)

TO DECORATE: Around centers of the flowers attached to tree branches, add the bulky yarn trim. Choose colors that complement the color of the felt. Sew on yarn over stitched area of flower. Overlap at bottom and let ends hang (Fig. 4). Repeat on other flowers.

Remove bastings and press entire grow chart, working carefully around the fluffy yarn areas.

MARKERS: For indicating height of the child at each birthday, it will be necessary to include "birthday markers." Use the flat backs of the buttons and numbers from the gold paper sheet. Lick number 1 and stick it on the button next to one hole, making sure holes are in position as shown in Fig. 5. This enables the parent to sew through the holes an arrow shape pointing to mark on tape measure that indicates child's height at age shown on the button. Repeat with number 2, etc., until each button has a number on it. The parent will sew one on each birthday.

5

Birthday markers

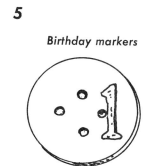

TO COMPLETE: Put these buttons in a small plastic bag along with the six 3" cardboard circles (to be used as backing for pictures). Tuck this bag into the pocket in the center back of the hem. Close with a tiny gold safety pin. Year after year, as the child grows, this pocket will hold the buttons until all are sewn in place.

Put a café-type curtain rod through the top hem to hang grow chart or tack it to the back of a door, bottom edge 3" above floor level.

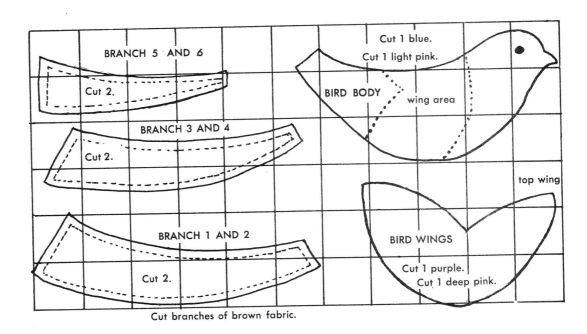

Cut branches of brown fabric.

PATTERNS FOR GROW CHART

(Each square = 1".)

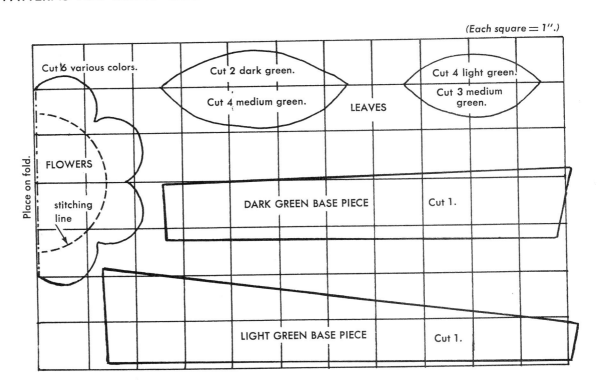

DUPLICATE the following instructions and include it with the gift, so the recipient knows how to complete and use the "family-tree grow chart". (Most public libraries have facilities for duplicating a page from a book.)

To make this grow chart your own personal family tree, find photographs of various generations of the child's family: sisters, brothers, parents, and grandparents. Cut the photographs to fit on the 3" cardboard circles in pocket in bottom hem. Glue picture to circle and glue circle inside large flowers on the tree. Put pictures of the older members of the family at the top.

Or the tree could also be used as a record of the child's development. Each year place a "birthday picture" in one of the flowers.

In the back pocket, you will find birthday markers, which should be kept in the pocket until used. On the child's birthday, let down the folded piece of tape measure so it hits the floor. Measure the child's height. Select a button with a number corresponding to the child's age at the current birthday. Then sew the button on the grow chart at mark on tape measure indicating the child's height. As you sew, you can create an arrow to point directly to the number indicating his height. Use heavy contrasting thread. Sew up through hole next to number, across to opposite hole, forming center line of arrow. Sew out from arrow point to other two holes creating arrow's head.

This will give you a permanent record of the child's height at each birthday.

Hang the chart so that bottom is 3" from floor.

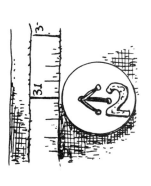

STUFFED LION

See color photograph following page 96.

This happy lion is designed to appeal to the toddler set but even a teen-ager would consider it a really great gift (especially one whose sign of the zodiac is Leo).

MATERIALS NEEDED

⅓ yd. any sturdy fabric (40″ wide) — fake fur, terry cloth, bonded fabric, velvet, corduroy

⅔ yd. wool or cotton blend upholstery fringe (2″ wide)

Thread to match fabric

Small bag of shredded foam for stuffing

Small pieces of felt: white for snout; black for lower nose and eyes; red for upper nose; green for eyes; orange for ears

Also needed: Felt marker, compass, paper for pattern

ENLARGE PATTERNS on opposite page. With compass, draw circle for head as indicated. Make separate patterns for snout and nose areas, and indicate placement on face pattern. Cut out patterns.

TO CUT: Lay patterns on wrong side of material (see Fig. 1 for placement on fabric). Flip body pattern for front and back. Pin in place.

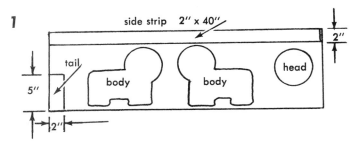

Cut pieces from wrong side of material. Cut small V shapes in curved sections as indicated on pattern. Keep cuts at least ⅛″ inside seam line. Cut the 2″ × 40″ side strip. For tail, cut a piece 5″ × 2″. If using corduroy, be sure the ribs are going the long way.

Cut face pieces out of felt as indicated on the pattern. For eyes, cut two ⅝″ circles of black and two ⅞″ circles of green (or cut around a nickel to make green circle, around a dime for black).

HEAD: Fold under at seam line, pin, and baste around the edge. Sew

PATTERN FOR STUFFED LION

(Each square = 1".)

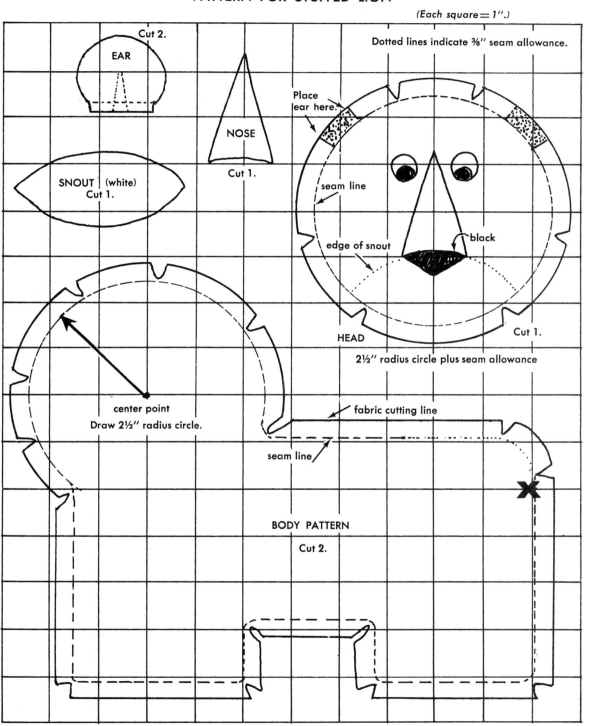

Cut 2.

EAR

NOSE

Cut 1.

SNOUT (white)
Cut 1.

Dotted lines indicate ⅜" seam allowance.

Place ear here.

seam line

edge of snout

black

HEAD

Cut 1.

2½" radius circle plus seam allowance

center point
Draw 2½" radius circle.

fabric cutting line

seam line

BODY PATTERN

Cut 2.

2

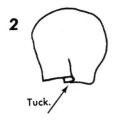

Tuck.

3

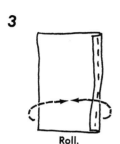

Roll.

4

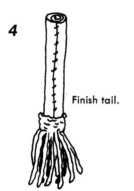

Finish tail.

face pieces in place before you assemble the toy. Sew white snout to lower face in position. Sew on red upper nose; then add black lower nose, slightly overlapping the red felt. Sew on eyes. (Or glue all features in position.)

Sew fringe all around face, about ⅛" in from edge. Ease it gently into proper position. Take a small tuck in base of each ear (Fig. 2). Sew ears in position.

TAIL: Baste ¼" under along one side. Roll other edge up to it, making a tight roll (Fig. 3) and sew together by hand. Sew a 2" piece of the fringe to the end of the rolled piece ¼" from end (Fig. 4).

TO ASSEMBLE BODY: Pin the strip to one body piece, right sides together. Leaving about ½", start pinning at point X on pattern. Go down and around legs and around body. There should be about 1" extra at end. Baste if desired, along the stitching line. Sew by machine, starting at X point and easing strip around corners. Sew around, ending at tail corner, leave about 1" unsewn (Fig. 5). Press seam.

Pin and stitch other body piece to the side piece aligning shape with piece already sewn. For an opening to turn fabric, stop stitching about 2½" from the tail end (Fig. 6). Turn right side out. Sew face to front, matching outside edges of head.

Fold under the 1" end of strip. Overlap other end of strip, insert end of tail between, and sew firmly in place (Fig. 7).

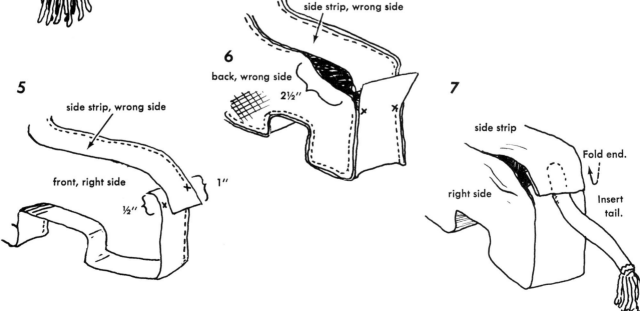

5 side strip, wrong side / front, right side / ½" / 1"

6 side strip, wrong side / back, wrong side / 2½"

7 side strip / right side / Fold end. / Insert tail.

STUFF lion with shredded foam (or use Dacron ® polyester fiberfill or cotton stuffing). For economy, cut old nylon stockings in pieces and use these for stuffing. Push stuffing into lion through the 2½" opening at back, then sew closed by hand, folding *in* the seam allowance. Remove any bastings.

VARIATION

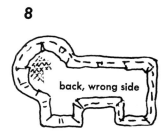

8

For a firmer shape to the lion, foam rubber can be used for stuffing. This foam is sold in some stores by the foot or in pieces for chair cushions. A 9" × 12" piece 1" thick is needed. Cut a paper pattern tracing inside dotted lines of body pattern. With a felt marker, trace around paper pattern onto the foam piece and cut out foam shape. Sew side strip to lion front as before. Sew on face and sew in tail. For back of lion, run a basting thread along stitching line so it will be visible on face of the fabric. Fold along this line and baste flat (Fig. 8). Insert the foam shape and fold side piece around the foam. Cut any notches needed to make fabric lay flat (Fig. 9). Lay the back piece in position onto folded-over side strip. Sew by hand along edge, making fabric fit snugly around the foam (Fig. 10). Remove bastings.

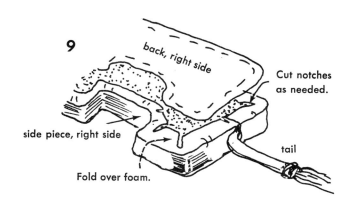

9

back, right side

Cut notches as needed.

side piece, right side

Fold over foam.

tail

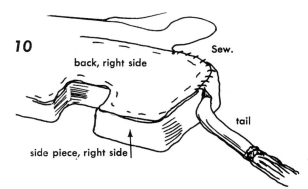

10

back, right side

Sew.

side piece, right side

tail

This basic lion pattern can be adapted to other animals and can be made of any fabric. Whimsical patterns on cotton fabric with a bright fringe make an attractive animal, too. The mane could be made of loops of yarn, sewn behind head, instead of fringe. If you have leopard-print or tiger-print fabric pieces, make the toy without the mane.

The size of the animal illustrated was kept small so that remnants or scraps could be used. This lion can be made much larger by scaling the pattern accordingly.

MERRY MENAGERIE HANGERS

Decorative hangers of just the right size for a tiny dress or coat are attractive and useful, and also serve as an amusing accessory for a child's room.

See color photograph following page 96.

MATERIALS NEEDED
(for bear and cat hangers)
Two regular-size hangers (wood) or two child-size hangers (wood or plastic)
4″ × 8″ tan fake fur, 4″ × 8″ white fake fur
Scraps of various-color fake fur, felts
Black embroidery floss and needle
Art foam 8″ × 8″, ⅛″ thick
10″ velvet tubing; white, pink, or blue
Paint, white latex, enamel finish
Also needed: Small handsaw, brush for paint, needle and matching threads

TO PREPARE BEAR HANGER: Saw about 1¾″ off each end of wooden hanger, leaving a piece about 12½″ long (Fig. 1). Sand ends smooth. Paint wooden part with white undercoat. After it dries, cover with enamel. Choose an appropriate color for a child's gift (yellow, white, light blue). Or use child-size plastic hanger as is.

FOR BEAR HEAD: Trace pattern. Cut two circles of tan fake fur. Pin pattern on back of fabric, cut from back. Cut two 3″ circles of art foam. For snout cut a 1⅝″ circle of yellow fake fur (or a 1⅜″ circle of felt). Trace the round-ear pattern, and cut two of brown felt. Cut eyes and nose of black felt.

Clip tan fur circles as shown on pattern, fold under edges ¼″ and baste around both circles.

FOR FACE: Turn under ⅛″ around edge of fur snout, and baste (not necessary for felt). Sew in position on one of the tan fur circles. Sew black felt eyes and nose in position. Make a small fold at base of each ear (Fig. 2). Sew ears in position behind face, against basted edge of fur (Fig. 3).

1

1¾″   12½″

2

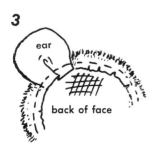

3

ear

back of face

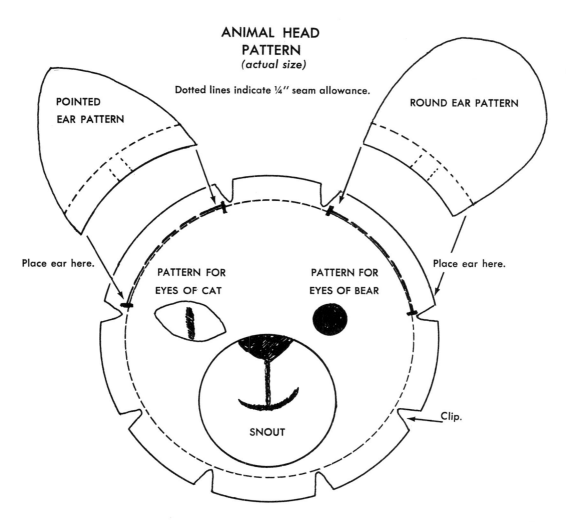

ANIMAL HEAD
PATTERN
(actual size)

Dotted lines indicate ¼″ seam allowance.

POINTED
EAR PATTERN

ROUND EAR PATTERN

Place ear here.

Place ear here.

PATTERN FOR
EYES OF CAT

PATTERN FOR
EYES OF BEAR

Clip.

SNOUT

TO ASSEMBLE: Slip a 5″ piece of velvet tubing over metal part of the hanger. Sew tip closed.

Make a sandwich of all pieces around the hanger as shown (Fig. 4): back fur piece, foam circle, hanger laid in place, other foam circle, and head placed on top, straight on hanger. Wooden "arms" will come out either side. Pin all together around hanger. Sew edges all around, going behind the ears, around the velvet tubing, sewing it in as you go. When reaching the wooden arm, sew firmly above wood, then run thread down inside fur and start sewing again below arm, taking extra stitches at first to hold around wood. Repeat on other side.

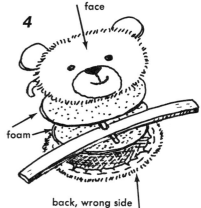

4

face

foam

back, wrong side

FOR CAT: The procedure is exactly the same, except that you will be using another color, ear shape will be pointed, and eyes almond-shaped. Make cat of yellow with pink or white snout. Embroider mouth on the snout before attaching to face.

VARIATIONS

Many animal faces can be made with these same basic patterns to create a merry menagerie. Variety is especially desirable if you want to give or sell these hangers as sets.

The faces below are half-size. To make, adapt the full-size pattern.

ANIMAL HEADS

LAMB
Use white fur face, black snout. Cut ears of black felt, using half of round ear shape.

RACCOON
On a grey fur face, add a white snout. Use black felt for mask, eyes, and ears (pointed ear shape, shortened).

LEOPARD (or tiger)
Patterned fake fur makes the animal's identity. Add yellow ears and snout, green eyes.

MOUSE
On grey fur, make a pink felt snout. Enlarge round ear shape, and cut it out of pink felt.

FOX
Make of red fur, brown felt snout, green eyes.

DOG
Make of brown or yellow fur. Add shaped brown felt ears.

6. GIFTS FOR BOYS AND GIRLS

As children reach school age, they begin to develop collector interests of their own. With this in mind, you can adapt for them many gifts described in other chapters. For instance, bookends (mentioned in Chapter 2) will please a child if decorated with pictures of cars, dolls, animals, bugs, space ships, etc. Carefully select these special-theme pictures and cut them from magazines, catalogs, or brochures. Attractive desk sets, including pencil holders that match, can be made by covering individual pieces with colorful, appropriate adhesive-backed vinyls. Pencil trays and boxes also can be covered with patterned gift papers. (See page 134.)

Presents for children are fun to make, and a joy to give. Remember to keep them simple, durable, and bright.

DRUM BANK

A popular theme for boys' rooms is early Americana: old maps, old soldier prints, etc. This drum bank should fit in and add to the décor.

MATERIALS NEEDED
Can with plastic top, 4″ diameter or less (This can held peanuts.)
1 yd. gold cord
2 yds. decorative gold rickrack
8 nailheads
1 gold-paper-foil eagle
Stars (from stationery store)
Paint, white latex and red enamel
Walnut stain, spray varnish
White glue or clear epoxy
Fabric glue or special glue to adhere to plastic
Also needed: Felt marker, brushes for paint and stain, clip clothespin, masking tape, utility knife or single-edged razor blade (to cut slit), rag (for stain)

See color photograph facing page 97.

1

TO PREPARE CAN: Remove cover. Give can a white latex undercoat. When dry, paint on red enamel. Add several coats of enamel, making sure each coat is dry before applying next one. Glue gold rickrack around base and top edge of can, keeping latter trim low enough so that the can's cover can be replaced. Apply two layers of rickrack, one on top of the other. Glue on eagle (Fig. 1) and scatter stars all around can. Spray on a coat of varnish.

When dry, cover with walnut stain. Allow to stand several minutes, then rub off. This gives an antiqued effect.

2

TO PREPARE NAILHEADS: Press prongs down and in (Fig. 2). Press all prongs to inside. Plan position of nailheads on can. They should be alternately spaced around, four on top and four on bottom (Fig. 3). Mark spots with felt-tipped pen.

3
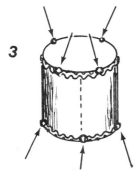

GOLD CORD will zigzag across can, caught by the nailheads top and bottom. Start at top, adding a little glue, and leaving a short end of cord. Glue to top. Add one nailhead over cord, and hold in place with a clip clothespin. Nailhead will remain over cord and nestled into rickrack.

When dry, bring cord down through next nailhead and glue in position on base, angling and pulling the cord so it is starting back up to top (Fig. 4). Hold in position with tape until dry. Then glue next nailhead on top. Let each dry as you continue around so you can pull against the last one to make cord taut.

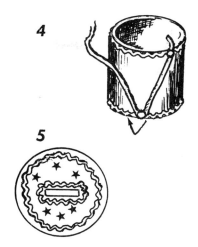

Zigzag cord back to start. Lift first nailhead slightly, pull cord through, glue. When this is dry, trim off ends.

TO FINISH: Cut a money slit 1½″ × ⅛″ in the plastic top. Using fabric or special glue, attach rickrack around outside edge and around slit (Fig. 5). Add some stars to top. When can is finished, add glue around edge of top and snap top in place.

"WHUFO"—A BEANBAG

The simple beanbag has been one of childhood's most beloved companions. This creature, with its "other planet" look, will surely charm today's boys and girls.

MATERIALS NEEDED
(for a beanbag approximately 5″ × 8″)
2 pieces, approximately 6″ × 9″ each, contrasting fabrics, sturdy texture
Piece of leather from chamois cloth or pieces of old gloves
2 small matching buttons for eyes
Dried peas or beans (¼ to ½ lb.)

See color photograph facing page 97.

ENLARGE PATTERNS: For back, pin paper body pattern (page 114) on fabric. Choose a fabric that is bright and fuzzy, such as fake fur or terry cloth. Cut out. For front, pin body pattern on a contrasting fabric, such as velvet or denim. (Use contrasting colors as well as contrasting textures.) Cut out. Using enlarged pattern, cut four "feet" out of the leather. Felt may be used instead but it is not as durable.

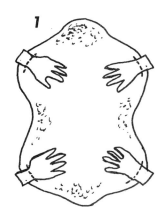

TO ASSEMBLE: Pin feet (toes pointing in) on the right side of the back, one at each corner (Fig. 1). Baste in place. Lay front piece right side

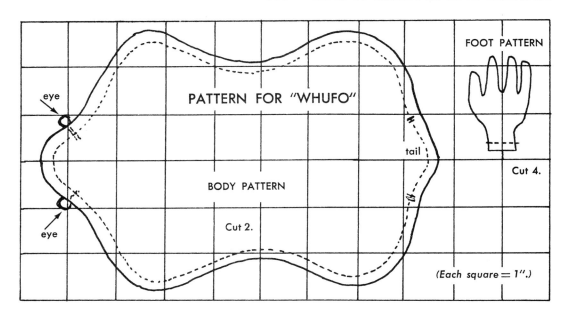

PATTERN FOR "WHUFO"

BODY PATTERN

Cut 2.

eye

eye

tail

FOOT PATTERN

Cut 4.

(Each square = 1".)

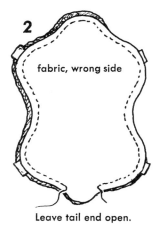

2

fabric, wrong side

Leave tail end open.

down, over the right side of the back and over the feet that have been basted in place. Pin the two body pieces together. Machine-stitch all around (allow ¼ ″ seam), leaving tail section open (Fig. 2). When you turn right sides out, feet should be in position.

INSERT DRIED PEAS OR BEANS until bag is about ¾ full. Pin tail closed and check whether creature is flexible enough to sit as shown. Remove some dried filling if "Whufo" is too stiff, or add more if needed. When you have the proper amount, turn in edges of open end and sew tail section closed. Stitch on button eyes.

GRENADIER RING TOSS

This ring-toss game offers a bonus as a decorative addition to a boy's room.

The royal guard is made of a plastic bottle whose shape suggests a grenadier. Choose one in blue, red, or yellow. Select a broomstick or dowel that fits tightly into the neck of the bottle. These are your basic components.

MATERIALS NEEDED

1 quart-size colored flexible plastic bottle (detergent or fabric-soft-
ener type)

Another bottle, the same color

One 9″ plastic disk (flying-saucer-type toy) or a 10″ square of wood
for base

⅝″ dowel (or whatever size fits through the neck of the bottle) or
broomstick, 21″ long

Package of gold-headed thumbtacks

Braid and edgings: 8″ gold loop braid; 4 ft. of gold and red braid,
gold soutache, red soutache; ½ yd. middy braid; plain string
or cord

½″ × 5″ black adhesive-backed vinyl

2″ square pink paper

Black paint (or color to match bottle), acrylic or enamel

1½″ pointed wood screw, washer to fit

¼″ thick rope and several thread spools. (Or 5″ or 6″ embroidery
hoops.)

Epoxy glue (or inquire at hardware store for best glue to attach
plastics)

White glue

Sand (enough to nearly fill bottle)

Also needed: Toothpicks, masking tape, screwdriver, felt pens—red
and black, awl (optional)

See color photograph facing page 97.

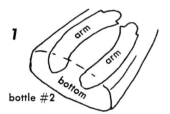

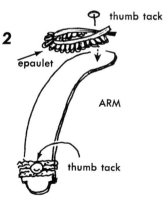

TRACE ARM PATTERN: Place pattern on bottom curve of second
bottle (Fig. 1). Cut from it one arm, flop pattern, cut other arm. Put two
layers of gold-red braid around ends of sleeves. Hold with thumbtack
(Fig. 2).

TO MAKE EPAULET: Cut a 4″ piece of loop braid, twisting around
until ends overlap each other. Push thumbtack through overlapped ends
(Fig. 2), then on down through top of arm piece. Repeat for other arm.

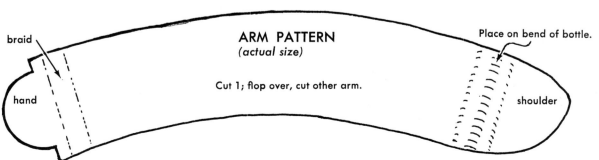

ARM PATTERN
(actual size)

Cut 1; flop over, cut other arm.

braid

hand

Place on bend of bottle.

shoulder

3 FACE PATTERN
(actual size)

TRACE FACE shape (Fig. 3). Transfer to pink paper. Draw features and hair with felt markers. Set aside.

TO DECORATE THE BOTTLE: Trim with braids to get a soldier's-uniform look that goes well with your particular bottle. To make leg separations, cut strips ¼″ × 5″ of black vinyl. Peel off backing and stick on front and back.

Now have fun decorating. For instance, crisscross red-gold braid across the chest, down to waist, with gold middy braid around waist. Push in thumbtacks to hold braids at waist and in center of chest and center of back. Cut piece of red middy braid long enough to go from waist on one side, around bottom of bottle, to waist on other side. Push thumbtack through all the braids at side of waist to hold in position (Fig. 4). Repeat on other side.

red-gold braid

red soutache   *Front*

TO ATTACH ARMS AND TRIMS: Mix a small amount of the epoxy glue. With a toothpick, slide glue under trims to secure in spots. Lift each thumbtack slightly, push epoxy glue into hole, under head of tack and under trim. Then replace tack in hole, pushing in firmly. Repeat until all thumbtacks and trims are glued in place. Add extra thumbtacks for decoration between braids, gluing in the same manner. Put two thumb-tacks at top of black vinyl in back (Fig. 5).

For arms, place epoxy glue around each thumbtack and under bent part of plastic at top of the arms. Make sure there is enough glue here. Set arms on shoulder, and push shoulder thumbtacks into bottle to secure arms in place.

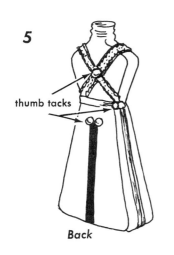

thumb tacks

Back

WEIGHTING: When glue is set and all pieces are firmly in place, fill bottle with sand. Work dowel down into sand until it hits the bottom of the bottle. So sand won't sift out while working, place some masking tape around top of bottle.

TO ATTACH BASE: Using awl, make pilot hole for screw in center of plastic disk, bottom of bottle, and center of wooden dowel inside bottle. Put screw through the washer, then screw through center of the 9″ plastic disk base. Continue screwing up into center bottom of bottle and into the center of the wooden dowel.

HEAD: Remove tape from top of bottle, add some white glue around neck, stuff cord or string down into any gap between neck and dowel to keep the sand inside. Glue face around stick with white glue. Glue gold cords and braids around, below face, as necessary to hide joining and screw threads of original bottle. This also makes a decorative neckline.

"HAT": Paint dowel black (or a color to match bottle) above the face. Glue on some middy braid for a visor, adding other trims as desired to decorate the very tall hat.

RINGS TO TOSS: Use old embroidery hoops painted a bright color, or make rings out of rope. Cut rope into 18″ lengths. Apply glue to ends and insert into spool. Make as many as desired. Numbers can be painted on the spools for special scoring.

ELEPHANT PAJAMA BAG

When collecting materials to make this whimsical pajama bag, keep your creative eyes open at all times. A fabric shop that takes orders for upholstery and slipcovers is a good source for the materials you'll need for this project. They sometimes have a "scrap basket" with odd-size pieces of fabrics of various textures and colors. If you are lucky, you may find a square that was originally part of a sample book of upholstery fabrics.

Should you be making items for a charity bazaar, some shops or manufacturers may donate fabric remnants. Friends often have pieces left over from home sewing projects.

See color photograph facing page 97.

MATERIALS NEEDED

Fabric: for pattern pieces A and B, ½ yd. of 40″ durable sturdy fabric (or a 32″ square)

for piece C (lining), 11″ × 15″ fabric or felt of contrasting color

for piece D, 9″ × 12″ pink felt

for ears, 9″ × 12″ felt or fabric, color to harmonize or contrast with fabric A

for tusks, 3½″ square of white felt

for headpiece, 4″ square bright-color felt (or fabric) to contrast with fabric A

2 black shank buttons, ½″ diameter, one 1″ diameter button

18″ decorative edging, ½″ wide

14″ gold braid or rickrack

3″ piece of round black elastic

Also needed: Thin paper (for patterns), pins, dressmaker tracing wheel and carbon (transfer sheet), thread

ENLARGE PATTERN for piece A (opposite page). Fold enlarged shape in half on center line to make sure both sides of pattern are alike, up to eye level. Open flat.

For pattern shape B, lay another piece of paper over pattern piece A that you have drawn. Trace along round end of A, measure up 13″ and draw line across. Add another 1½″ above this line (see opposite page).

For pattern piece C, lay another piece of paper over pattern A. Trace trunk end, measure up 15″ from trunk tip, draw line across.

Enlarge mouth shape for pattern D. Cut out. Align straight edges and center on pattern B. Trace around D as guide for placement of mouth on B.

Enlarge ear and tusk patterns. Mark on edge of pattern A where ears will attach. Mark placement of eyes. Check all patterns to make sure contours match where necessary. Cut out patterns.

PIN PATTERNS: Place patterns A and B on the large piece of basic fabric. Cut out. With a dressmaker's wheel and transfer sheets, indicate placement of eyes, mouth, tusks, and ears. Mark fold-over line. Position of pieces can also be indicated with pins or by basting through pattern and tearing pattern away from fabric.

Pin pattern C (trunk lining) on fabric or felt and cut out. Pin pattern D (mouth) on pink felt and cut out. For ears, pin pattern on felt (or fabric) and cut two. Cut two more ears out of basic fabric or a contrasting fabric. Cut two tusks of white felt. For head decoration, cut a 4″ square of fabric or felt. Use whatever color combinations you choose.

ATTACH HEAD DECORATION before assembling bag. Pin square in position, centering on head (piece A), and aligning corners of square with fold line (Fig. 1). Sew on by machine (or use fabric glue to attach piece). Sew, or glue, decorative edging along edge of headpiece and gold rickrack about 1″ from edges of headpiece (Fig. 1), or ornament as desired.

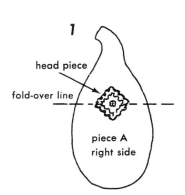

1

head piece

fold-over line

piece A
right side

PATTERN FOR ELEPHANT PAJAMA BAG

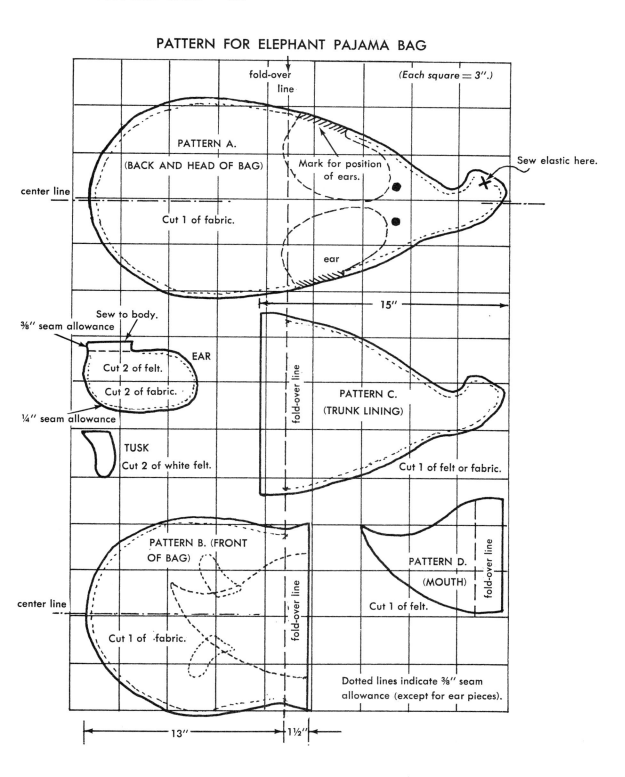

(Each square = 3".)

fold-over line

PATTERN A.

(BACK AND HEAD OF BAG)

Mark for position of ears.

Sew elastic here.

center line

Cut 1 of fabric.

ear

Sew to body.

⅜" seam allowance

EAR

Cut 2 of felt.

Cut 2 of fabric.

¼" seam allowance

TUSK

Cut 2 of white felt.

15"

fold-over line

PATTERN C.

(TRUNK LINING)

Cut 1 of felt or fabric.

PATTERN B. (FRONT OF BAG)

center line

Cut 1 of fabric.

fold-over line

PATTERN D.

(MOUTH)

fold-over line

Cut 1 of felt.

Dotted lines indicate ⅜" seam allowance (except for ear pieces).

13"   1½"

2

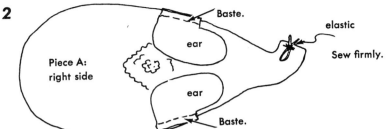

Piece A: right side

ear

ear

Baste.

Baste.

elastic

Sew firmly.

3

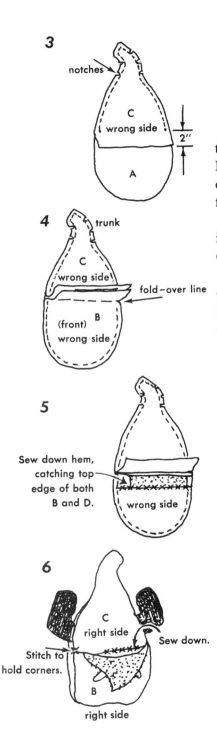

notches →

C
wrong side

2"

A

4

trunk

C
wrong side

fold-over line

(front)
B
wrong side

5

Sew down hem, catching top edge of both B and D.

wrong side

6

C
right side

Sew down.

Stitch to hold corners.

B

right side

EARS AND TRUNK LINING: Lay an ear of felt and an ear of fabric together, right sides facing, and pin. Repeat, making a right and left ear. Machine-sew around edges, making a ¼″ seam. Leave the ⅜″ seam area open to attach to body (see pattern). Turn ears right side out and press flat.

Pin ears on right side of piece A (Fig. 2). Baste in place. Fold elastic in half. Sew at center point of trunk at seam line. Loop must be facing in (point X, pattern A).

Pin trunk lining (piece C) in place over ears and elastic, matching edges of trunk. Sew lining to trunk and head by machine (⅜″ seam), leaving 2″ on each side seam unsewn (Fig. 3). Be careful not to catch the finished edges of the ears in the seam as you sew.

Cut a few notches in the seam where trunk curves (Fig. 3). (Do not cut into the stitching.)

TUSKS AND MOUTH: Place tusks and sew in place on front (piece B). Position and pin mouth (piece D) according to pattern. (Tip of mouth should show when trunk is folded down.) Mouth and tusks can be appliquéd to front by hand or machine. Pin top edge of D to edge of B.

TO ATTACH FRONT OF BAG: Lay piece B on piece A with right sides together. Align edges and pin. Starting 1½″ down from the corner on front, machine-stitch down and around bag, stopping 1½″ from end at fold line marked on pattern (Fig. 4). Front and trunk lining should almost meet, with hem of each unstitched

TO FINISH FRONT (PIECE B): Pin the 1½″ fold over (including edge of D). Sew in place, using a catch stitch to form a hem (Fig. 5).

TURN both sections of the bag right side out. Turn under loose edge of trunk lining (piece C) and sew by hand (Fig. 6) to back of bag. Make some extra stitches at each corner where the fabrics meet, so front and back won't pull apart.

EYES: Sew ½" buttons onto piece A (see pattern for placement). If your material is dark, cut two ¾" circles of white felt and sew on first, then sew button in center of each.

BAG FASTENING: Fold trunk down over the pajama bag. Elastic loop should be protruding from end of trunk. Mark position for the button (Fig. 7). Sew the large button at this point.

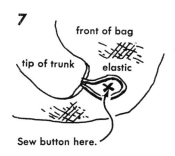

VARIATIONS

Although pajama bags are generally made for young children, teen-agers love them to decorate their beds. Make this elephant in wild colors or patterned fabrics, fake leather, fur, or shiny vinyl, to appeal to the older age group.

JOLLY JINGLE BIRD PUPPET

Plan to make this jester bird for the school-age child, old enough to manipulate the bird and put on performances. (It's not intended for tiny tots, who might pry loose the bells.)

See color photograph facing page 97.

MATERIALS NEEDED

10" square piece of stretch fabric, such as cotton jersey (yellow) or bottom of sock with heel cut off.

Two 8" × 10" pieces of sturdy fabric, pink and green (or scraps, prints or plain)

6" × 8" pink felt

Five ½" jingle bells

2 sew-on eyes, ½" in diameter (from craft-supply), or black buttons, or felt for eyes.

18" bulky yarn, bright green (hair or gift-tie)

3" diameter ball; hollow rubber ball or a semi-rigid "practice" plastic baseball (with holes) or styrofoam ball.

Two yellow plastic spoons

1½" ring (a rubber washer, or metal curtain ring)

5 ordinary pipe cleaners (cut 3½" long each)

Also needed: Fabric glue, clip clothespins, knife, tongs, small pan, transparent tape

1

beak decoration

slit (to slip over beak)

2

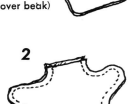

PATTERNS AND CUTTING: On paper, enlarge the patterns below for half-body and comb. Place body pattern on fold of pink fabric. Cut front. Place pattern on fold of green, cut back of puppet. Using comb pattern, cut two pieces of pink felt.

TO MAKE DECORATION AROUND BEAK: Cut a 1¾″ × 1″ piece of pink felt. Cut a ½″ slit in center of this piece (Fig. 1) and round the corners.

BODY: Pin the pink and green body pieces, right sides together, and stitch by machine up the sides and around the arms, allowing ¼″ seams. Leave bottom and neck open (Fig. 2). By hand, sew a rolled hem around bottom edge (or glue hem). Turn body right side out. Turn ½″ down inside neck, baste.

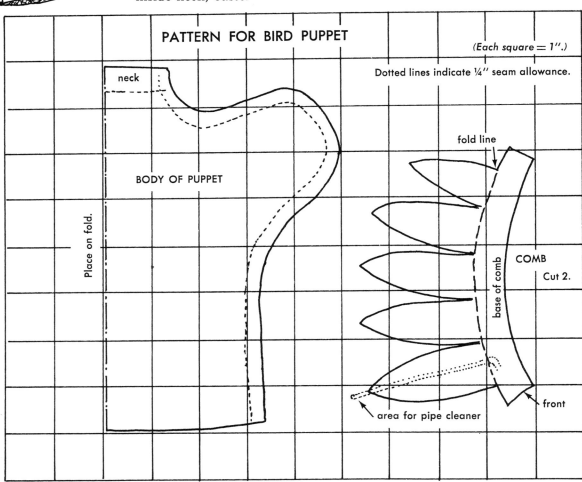

PATTERN FOR BIRD PUPPET

(Each square = 1″.)

Dotted lines indicate ¼″ seam allowance.

neck

BODY OF PUPPET

Place on fold.

fold line

base of comb

COMB

Cut 2.

area for pipe cleaner

front

3

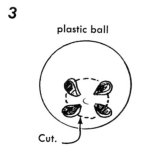

plastic ball

Cut.

4

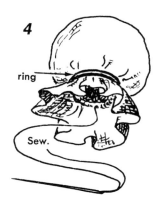

ring

Sew.

5

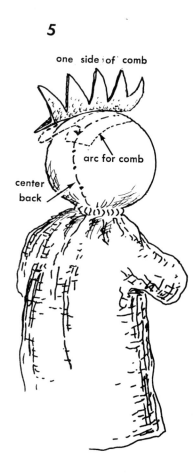

one side of comb

arc for comb

center back

HEAD: Cut a 1½" hole in the rubber ball to allow place for finger when animating puppet. If you use a plastic ball, cut hole with a heated knife (Fig. 3). If using a styrofoam ball, use a grapefruit knife to hollow out area for fingers.

TO COVER HEAD: Use the stretch fabric and the 1½" ring. Stretch the piece of fabric around the ball and through the ring. Ring should be in position around finger hole (Fig. 4). Sew stretch fabric to the ring, sewing in and out to hold. Trim off excess fabric, leaving at least ½" below the ring. Sew neck edges of body to fabric of head just above ring.

COMB: Mark off a center line on the head, from center forehead to center neck in the back. Measure out ½" either side of center line as a guide to sew edge of base of each comb piece (Fig. 5). Fold out base of one comb piece and pin base on one side of center guideline. Repeat for other comb piece. Points of comb should meet and stand up. Glue and sew down the base of both comb pieces, leaving open points sticking up.

Place pipe cleaners inside of points of the comb, and bend where pipe cleaner touches the head (Fig. 6). (There will be more to bend toward the back of comb where points are shorter.) Pipe cleaners should protrude about ½" above tips of points. Using fabric glue, attach pipe cleaners to center area in head. Glue two points of felt together with pipe cleaner between (Fig. 7). Hold with clothespins until dry. Pipe cleaners make the comb stand up.

When glue is dry, slip bell over the tip of pipe cleaner that is sticking out, twist end in, and sew to hold. Sew and glue eyes in position.

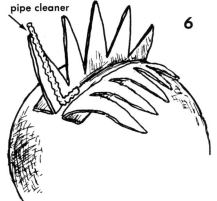

pipe cleaner

6

bell

7

pipe cleaner
glued between

8

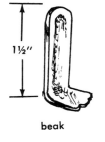

1½″

beak

BEAK: Break off ends of the two plastic spoons (or forks), leaving about 2¼″ of the handle. Hold handle with tongs and immerse broken end in a pan of hot water until the plastic softens slightly. Press end against the bottom of the pan to form a right angle about 1½″ from the tip (Fig. 8). Repeat, bending the other handle end.

Add some fabric glue under bent ends and place both pieces in position on head, as shown (Fig. 9). Temporarily hold tips with tape. Sew a few stitches across each base to hold. Add glue to the felt piece, slide over beaks, down against face. This holds and hides the base of the beak (Fig. 10). Sew around edge of felt to secure. Remove tape.

TO COMPLETE: Tie yarn around neck, adding a dab of glue at tips of yarn so it won't ravel.

VARIATIONS
This jingle bird can be made of fabric scraps (sturdy cottons or bonded fabrics are best). The sillier the color combinations, the better. Comb should be of felt.

9

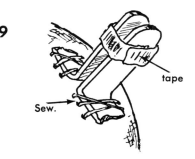

tape

Sew.

10

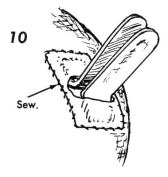

Sew.

7. ZINGY GIFTS FOR TEENS

If you would appeal to the young, you must be sharply attuned to their scene, since most teen-agers follow fads and trends with a zeal brief but intense. In planning gifts for them, you should be aware of the newest craze and, utilizing craft techniques, adapt them to the latest styles. Explore fashion and teen magazines for timely accessory ideas.

To make gifts that teen-agers really enjoy, let yourself go, be inventive, daring, and colorful. Don't shy away from brilliant fluorescent tones, shiny silver, or improbable color combinations.

Much of the renewed interest in crafts today stems from youthful imagination. Disenchanted with machine-made items, the young *do* appreciate handwork and are receptive to creative uses for commonplace objects.

In this book, perhaps, they too will discover ideas and craft techniques they can apply when making their own things.

FLOUR-CLAY JEWELRY

Jewelry for teens should be exciting—the more offbeat, the better. Who knows what idea may start a new fad? These suggestions for jewelry made of flour clay, for instance. See color photograph facing page 136.

MATERIALS NEEDED

Flour clay (see page 33 for the recipe)

Hairpins, wire jump links, chains, cords, purchased pin-back, jewelry catches, seed beads, old beads, etc.

Beading wire, nylon fishing line

Paint: fluorescent, acrylic, spray-on paint, metallics, rub-on, etc.

Also needed: Small hand drill, brush, heavy scissors or wire cutters (for cutting hairpins), plastic straw, toothpick, buttons, or other tools to indent shapes in clay

(Select what you need from these materials for the piece you make.)

PREPARE CLAY: Homemade flour clay is easy to work with, and is versatile besides. Clay should be rolled out at least ⅛ ʺ thick, but not more than ¼ ʺ. Keep finished thickness of piece about ¼ ʺ for most work.

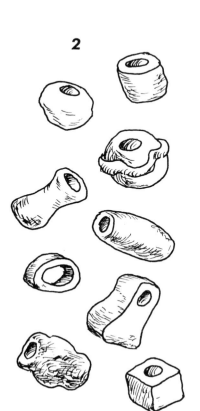

SHAPING: This clay molds into very tiny pieces which will stick firmly to each other after baking. You can roll thin little "snakes" or tiny balls to lay on a background for good effects (Fig. 1). Surface can be indented by gently pressing a textured shape with a decorative button, then removing the button. Experiment with other objects that might give an interesting texture to the surface.

Since clay expands slightly as it is baked, any embedded object remains firmly in place. Any number of little things can be added to make the jewelry more interesting—marbles, nails, seashells, etc. Just make sure such pieces can take the heat when the clay is baked. Glass, metal, and wood (no plastic) are the best materials for this purpose.

SUGGESTIONS FOR FINISHING AND PAINTING: After baking, be as far-out as you like in decorating the clay pieces. Cover with two coats of fluorescent or acrylic paint (allow to dry between coats). Using brush, *lay on* the paint gently, don't work it around. When dry, it has an interesting surface. Another method is to finish with several light coats of metallic or bright colored spray-on paint. Raised details can be painted a contrasting color with acrylic paint. Or a "rub-on" finish can be sparingly applied over the base color for a dimensional effect.

Most paints will last longer and look better if given a finish of spray-on varnish or plastic spray. The following are ideas for specific jewelry shapes.

BEADS

TO MAKE BEADS: Roll flour clay into balls. Beads can be shaped into a variety of forms (Fig. 2), but should be limited to a ¾″ diameter or less. For tiny beads, too small for a hole, insert a fine wire in the bead when it is rolled (Fig. 3). (After baking, assemble by twisting wire around a jump link or wire loop.) Be careful not to overbake small pieces.

TO STRING BEADS AFTER BAKING: Make holes with a small hand drill. Paint or color as your wish. Beads can be strung in many ways. Nylon fishing line is excellent for stringing, because of its strength and transparency. Bulky beads can be strung on colorful yarn or a leather thong, with knots between, leaving spaces of yarn or thong showing (Fig. 4), or you can alternate flour beads with purchased or old beads.

You may add a pendant to a string of beads. Using fishing line, tie to one side of clasp and string beads (Fig. 5). After stringing enough beads for half of necklace, string on three decorative beads and go through loop in pendant top (Fig. 6). Then go back through the three decorative beads (Fig. 7). Now continue stringing other half of necklace and tie securely to remaining side of clasp. Push line back through last few beads and cut off (Fig. 8). Do the same on other side of clasp. To secure, you may add a tiny drop of glue to the knot. This method of stringing can be used to add as many dangles as desired.

PINS AND PENDANTS

A basic shape can be adapted to pendant or pin.

TO MAKE A PIN: Use a purchased pin-back. When jewelry shape has been made, turn over and press pin back into the clay very slightly. Roll two strips of clay and press over back bar of pin-back. Keep strips away from pin ends, since the clay will expand slightly when baked. If it should expand in the wrong place, after baking, chip away a few pieces (with a small paring knife) so pin will work.

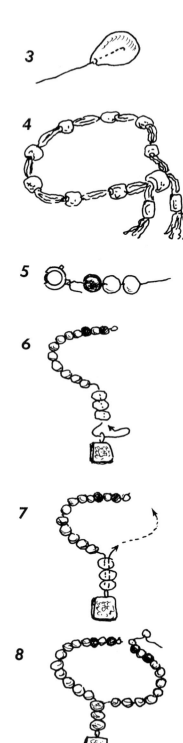

TO MAKE A PENDANT: Make a hole in top of shape using the end of a plastic straw. Or make a hanging loop of wire, by using a fine wire hairpin. Cut hairpin just below first kink (Fig. 9). Insert ends into the clay before baking. These loops are also helpful if you plan to suspend other beads from the bottom of a pendant, or would like to assemble a necklace using jump links (Fig. 10).

After painting, pendants can be suspended from purchased chains, cords, leather thongs, narrow velvet ribbon, beads on a string, etc.

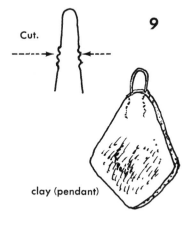

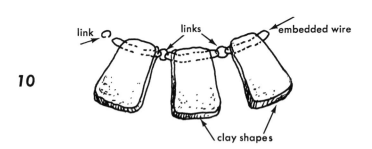

OTHER USES FOR CLAY JEWELRY SHAPES

CHOKERS: Make a pin or pendant shape with a hole on each side. Sew to a ribbon. Or, string beads to the proper length for a choker with catch in back.

BRACELETS: String beads on elastic thread.

BELTS: You can also make units for decorative belts, with holes on either side. Thread cord, ribbon or thongs through holes (Fig. 11). Tie in front.

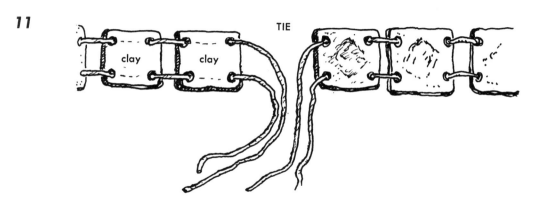

VARIATIONS

Create whatever jewelry suits your whims and the fashions of the day.
Stores and magazines will give you ideas that adapt well to the flour-clay
technique. Pictured below are a few suggestions.

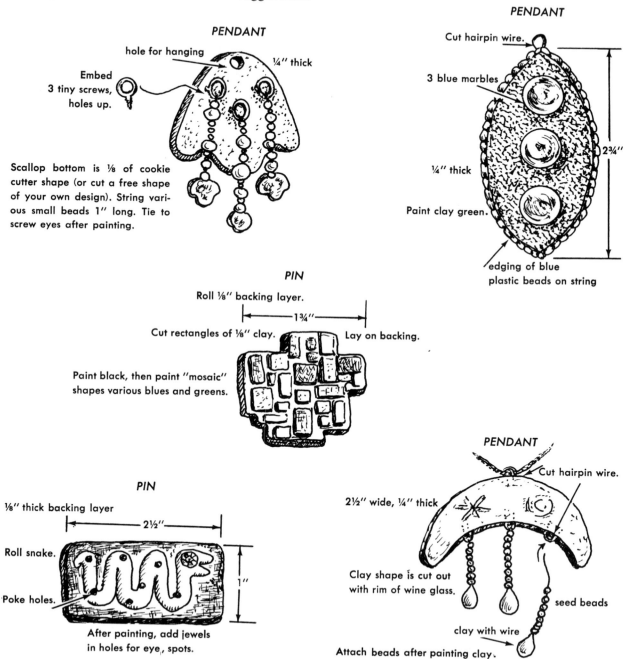

PENDANT

hole for hanging

¼" thick

Embed
3 tiny screws,
holes up.

Scallop bottom is ⅛ of cookie
cutter shape (or cut a free shape
of your own design). String various small beads 1" long. Tie to
screw eyes after painting.

PENDANT

Cut hairpin wire.

3 blue marbles

¼" thick

Paint clay green.

2¾"

edging of blue
plastic beads on string

PIN

Roll ⅛" backing layer.

1¾"

Cut rectangles of ⅛" clay.   Lay on backing.

Paint black, then paint "mosaic"
shapes various blues and greens.

PIN

⅛" thick backing layer

2½"

Roll snake.

1"

Poke holes.

After painting, add jewels
in holes for eye, spots.

PENDANT

Cut hairpin wire.

2½" wide, ¼" thick

Clay shape is cut out
with rim of wine glass.

seed beads

clay with wire

Attach beads after painting clay.

NAIL JEWELRY

*See color photograph
facing page 136.*

MATERIALS NEEDED

Two 1½" and three 2½" flooring nails (square ends)
One 1" flat metal washer
Four ¼" rings or jump links
Six fake jewels for trim (or pearls or beads)
Silver rub-on finish
Dull black spray paint, spray-on varnish
Epoxy putty, epoxy glue
Jewelry findings: silver-colored earring backs (or ear wires for
    pierced ears), with loop for pendant drops, jump links
Silver chain for pendant (or leather cord)
Also needed: Fine sandpaper, small knife

PENDANT AND EARRINGS

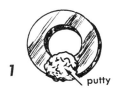

1   *putty*

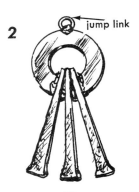

2   jump link

3

Indent.

TO PREPARE: Clean tips of all the nails with fine sandpaper. Glue adheres best to raw metal. Mix the epoxy putty according to directions on can.

TO ASSEMBLE PENDANT: Place washer on flat surface. Add putty as shown (Fig. 1). Lay three 2½" nails over washer and push down into the putty, spacing properly (Fig. 2). Remove excess putty with tip of a clean knife. Put a dab of putty on top of washer to secure the jump link to the piece. Make a small ball of putty about ¼" around. Dab on end of a nail, flatten it slightly, then make an identation in it. Later you will glue a "jewel" into this indentation. Repeat on other two nails and in center where nails meet (Fig. 3).

EARRINGS: Put a dab of putty at end of each 1½" nail, and indent as before, to place jewel. Add just enough putty at point of nail to attach the jump link (Fig. 4).

TO FINISH: Allow putty to set overnight. When putty is firm and hard, and all pieces are secure, spray black. Allow to dry.
With a silver rub-on type finish, highlight the jewelry very lightly. Pieces should still look black but have a glow of silver on the edges and a slight silver shine on the high parts.

With epoxy glue (or household cement), glue jewels into the indentations. Give pieces a coat of clear nail polish or varnish to prevent color coming off on clothing.

Attach earring by slipping the jump ring into the ring of the earring back (Fig. 5).

Attach pendant with a jump link through the glued-on ring, and link to chain.

4

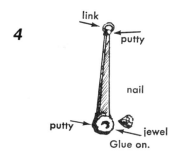

VARIATIONS

Jewelry made of nails is also effective without the jewels. Use the putty only in spots necessary to hold piece together. Rub silver on nail tips as a highlight. Brown with rub-on gold is equally striking. Any color combination can be used, brilliant or subdued. Or paint nails with bright enamel. Glue on metal stars or charms.

You can also make attractive pins using this process. Sand edges of four 2½" nails so raw metal shows. Lay flat. Apply putty over back and between nails. Push in purchased pin-back. When set, finish as before. Glue jewel or trim in front (Fig. 6).

5

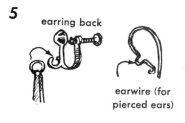

6   PIN

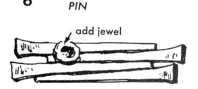

HINGE BELT

Functional everyday hinges with gracefully curved edges can be transformed into a handsome belt.

MATERIALS NEEDED

1 yd. brown grosgrain ribbon, 1½" wide (or width needed to fit hinges used)

2 sets of hinges, gold or brass-colored, about 1¼" high

2 gold-colored sash rod curtain brackets

1 yd. brown cord

Package of cluster beads, green

Gold seed beads

Also needed: Pliers, fabric glue, brown thread

See color photograph facing page 136.

TO ASSEMBLE BELT: Cut grosgrain ribbon 27" long (or length of waist measurement needed). Fold under ¾" and hem both ends. Space

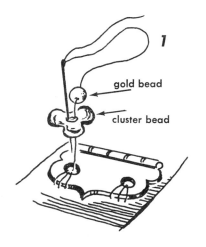

gold bead

cluster bead

the four hinges evenly along the length of the ribbon. Attach to the ribbon by sewing on with brown thread. Stitch through screw holes where sewing will show the least. For decoration, and also to help hold hinges in place, add beads. Go up through screw hole again (Fig. 1), through a cluster bead, through a seed bead, down through the cluster bead and back through the same screw hole. Pull thread tight. Repeat on all the screw holes to attach all the hinges.

CLOSING: Attach one sash rod bracket to one end of belt (Fig. 2). Sew on through screw holes, then sew on beads as before. Cut brown cord in half. Fold each piece in half. Slip one piece into the bracket. With pliers, press metal tip down, closing it over the center of the cord. This prevents cord from slipping. Repeat on other end. To keep tips of cord from fraying, dip ends in a little glue.

TO WEAR: Tie double cords together in front.

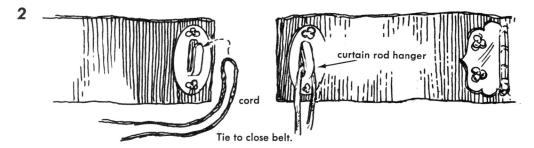

cord

Tie to close belt.

curtain rod hanger

VARIATIONS

For a heavier, wider belt, add a felt backing ⅛″ wider than ribbon on each side. Attach by sewing along ribbon edge as neatly as possible. Or glue ribbon to a leather strip of desired width. Sew brackets through both ribbon and leather.

HANGING JEWELRY BOARD

Make an eye-catching gift that solves the problem of tangled jewelry by hanging chains, belts, beads, pendants, and bracelets on one decorative board.

MATERIALS NEEDED

10″ × 14″ piece of pine wood, ¾″ thick (or a rectangular cutting board, even an old one)

½ yd. adhesive-backed vinyl, appropriate design

Various "fun" hooks: bright-colored ceramic clothes hook, small spool, old wire clothes hooks, old knobs, old doorstops (any screw-in shape on which chains can be hung)

12″ × 15″ piece of corrugated cardboard (optional)

2 screw-in type picture hangers

1½ yds., ¾″ wide, edging (grosgrain ribbon or decorative braid)

Black paint, bright paint (to finish old hardware)

Also needed: White glue, fabric glue, awl, screwdriver

See color photograph facing page 136.

PREPARE BOARD: If you use an old cutting board, clean thoroughly. If using pine, sand smoothly. Cut a piece of adhesive-backed vinyl ½″ larger than the board all around. Peel off backing and stick to the board. Press down. Clip corners and fold down over edges.

Decide on placement of hangers. (See suggested placement in Fig. 1.) On a board this size you can use about six units. They should be set in a staggered pattern, so that long chains hanging from upper hooks will not hit lower hooks.

PREPARE HANGERS: Remove the rubber tip from doorstop. For the bent type doorstop (Fig. 2), add a small spool on tip. If necessary, enlarge hole in one end of spool with the tip of a sharp knife. Apply glue to inside of hole and insert doorstop into spool (or add a large cork).

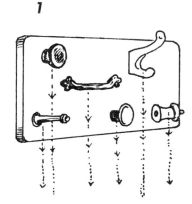

PAINT any old hardware or knobs in bright colors.

ASSEMBLE when all units are painted and dry. Set one hook in position. Make a small hole with an awl. Screw in hook. Repeat with all units, screwing them firmly in place.

If any of the screws are longer than the thickness of the wood, and protrude in back, it will be necessary to cover the back. Cut a piece of corrugated cardboard the exact size of the board, and glue to back. (If screws protrude more than ¼″, they will have to be sawed or cut off before you cover back with cardboard.)

TO FINISH: Paint back and edges black. When dry, use fabric glue to attach the ribbon (or edging) around the edges, hiding the corrugations of the cardboard and the edge of the vinyl. Screw two hanger hooks in top.

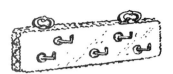

VARIATIONS

This colorful board was planned for a teen-ager's room, but its practicality would endear it to almost any woman. For a daintier version, use a smaller board, about 2″ × 7″, and cover with velour, velvet, or other appropriate background. Using fabric glue, attach fabric to board. Screw in five gold hanging hooks, similar to cup hooks (Fig. 3). Trim side edges with braid to match fabric (or gold braid). Screw decorative hangers into top edge.

See color photograph facing page 136.

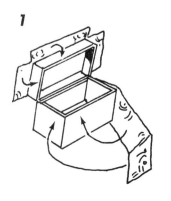

DESK ACCESSORIES

To add a fresh look to ordinary desk accessories, cover them with brilliantly designed gift-wrap paper.

MATERIALS NEEDED
Gift-wrap paper (Select good quality and appropriate design, as for example: a fluorescent green with modern black pattern.)
Square-sided box (old or new)
Styrofoam or papier-mâché tray approximately 3½″ × 8½″ × 1″ (from the supermarket)
Bottle
Middy braid (black)
White glue, fairly thin; styrofoam glue
Black acrylic paint (brush or spray)
Varnish, high gloss

BOX

TO COVER BOTTOM SECTION OF THE BOX: Cut gift-wrap paper in approximate height and length needed. Open box. Add glue to back of paper. Place paper on box (Fig. 1), aligning straight edge of paper with opened edge of box. Fold around, press down. Overlap about ¼″ in back. When dry, trim bottom edge even.

TO COVER TOP SECTION: Draw pattern on back of the paper. Set top of box on paper, draw around. Extend lines. Measure height of lid. Draw this dimension on the paper for covering lid sides. Allowing a little extra for folds, cut out. Glue on top and sides. Press down so paper is smooth. Trim off any excess. Glue middy-braid edging along lower edge of cover.

VASE

PREPARE BOTTLE: Choose a bottle that is somewhat vase-shaped. The side should be straight and smooth so that paper can be glued on easily (Fig. 2). Paint the top of the bottle black. If the bottom is curved, paint this area black, too.

TO MAKE A PATTERN: Cut a piece of scrap paper and wrap around area of bottle you will cover. Trim paper to get general idea of shape you will need. Cut this shape from the gift-wrap paper, allowing for overlap.

TO ATTACH: Smooth glue over bottle, lay paper on and smooth around, sliding paper until it fits the area to be covered. Trim off excess (Fig. 3).

ADD TRIM when glue is dry. Glue middy braid at edge of paper. Since the braid is fairly wide, it will hide any unevenness where paper was cut. Glue middy braid (or cord) around top to hide the ridges and make this look more like a vase.

PENCIL TRAY

PREPARE TRAY: Use a papier-mâché supermarket fruit tray. Paint outside black, using acrylic paint. (If tray is styrofoam, don't use an oil-base paint.)

TO CUT PAPER: Trace around base of tray on back of gift-wrap paper. Measure the height of the walls of the tray. Add this dimension to the base area, making four side panels (Fig. 4). Draw notches at paper corners. Cut out and fit paper down inside tray. Cut notches wider, if necessary, so it will fit without too many folds (Fig. 5). Remove paper.

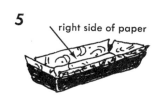

TO ASSEMBLE: Add styrofoam glue to tray and glue paper down inside, adding glue where paper overlaps. Trim off edges and smooth as much as possible. Glue middy braid around the top edge.

TO FINISH ALL PIECES: Allow to dry, then varnish with the shiniest varnish or plastic coating you can find. Use several coats for durability as well as high gloss.

VARIATIONS

Make other desk accessories to match. Cover sides of a purchased desk pad or a small box of drawers. Letter baskets, wastebaskets, pencil caddy, bookends, etc., have been discussed in Chapter 4. Give these projects a "young" look by covering them with appropriate paper.

Other sources of covering materials include wallpapers with "wet look" in brilliant colors, or adhesive-backed vinyls, or burlap. An old poster might be used. Some posters have intricate backgrounds, often in fluorescent colors. With fabric glue, it is possible to use some types of lightweight colorful fabrics or fake leathers.

BLOB BATIK

One of the oldest means of creating patterns on fabric, when being dyed, was called the "resist" method. A substance, added to the fabric, repelled or resisted the dye, and this created the patterns.

To make traditional batik, heated wax is applied with various tools to sections of the cloth. Then the cloth is dyed, other areas are waxed, and the cloth is dyed again. The wax resists the dye. This produces intricate designs. True batik is tedious, requiring considerable skill, experience, and patience. Blob batik is a short-cut method for making bright, contemporary, abstract patterns.

MATERIALS NEEDED
24″ square of white fabric (preferably cotton or linen)
Package of household wax (paraffin)
1 box each of fuchsia pink and deep purple fabric dyes
Yellow wax crayon
Also needed: Large wooden spoon, bowl scraper, newspapers, pan (for dye bath), brush (optional)

Hanging from Jewelry Board (page 132): Flour-clay Pendants (page 126); Hinge Belt (page 131); Glass Pendants (page 50). On the table: Nail Jewelry (page 130)—Pendant (far left) and Earrings (far right); Glass Pin (page 51); Flour-clay Pin (page 127); Covered Box (page 134)

Christmas Ornaments of Flour Clay (page 32); Plastic Angel Ornaments (page 35); Plastic Easter Eggs (page 30)

PREPARE FABRIC: If fabric is new, wash to remove sizing, and press if necessary. Using the yellow crayon, scribble color on the fabric, with some idea of a design in mind. You might make some simple "suns" in each corner of the fabric, adding a circular scribble in the center (Fig. 1). Lay the crayon on heavily and don't worry about the shapes—they won't show much in the end. Use up most of the crayon.

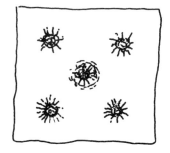

1

TO MAKE A "PUSHER TOOL": Remove the rubber part from a bowl scraper. The remaining piece is a sturdy-handled tool.

MELT THE WAX in a double boiler, being careful *none* gets near the flame. *Never* heat wax directly over the heat, for it is very flammable.

Spread newspaper on the table in a wide area larger than your fabric, since you probably will spill some wax. Spread fabric out flat on the papers.

Remove wax from stove when liquid, but leave in the double boiler over the hot water, to keep wax in liquid form as long as possible. If wax starts to thicken, reheat.

TO APPLY WAX: With a large spoon, drop, drip, and carefully splash the wax on the fabric. To create basic design, start by blobbing wax over the "suns" you drew, covering them as much as possible. Sprinkle and flip spots of wax over the rest of the fabric freely. But be very careful not to splash the wax on you or those around you. You'll soon learn to control the wax so it lands on the fabric in blobs as small or big as you desire. Splashes become effective designs, so enjoy yourself. Abstracts have no rules, and each design is unique.

Use the "pusher tool" to keep wax from piling up too much in certain spots. Shove wax over or around while still soft. Or scoop up excess wax and return to the pot if too deep in any spot. Wax merely has to saturate the surface to create patterns. Leave many areas of the fabric untouched; this is where the dye will take.

TO DYE: Use about ¼ of the fuchsia pink dye mixing dye according to instructions. (For stronger colors, use about ½ package to pint of water.) Pick up the fabric and immerse it in cool water. While it is in the water, crush it lightly with your hands to cause small cracks in the wax. The fine lines of the cracking will allow the dye to penetrate, creating the batik effect.

Place fabric in pan of *cool* dye. (Do not place in hot dye; it melts the

2

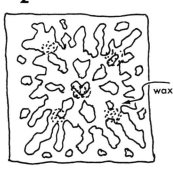

wax

wax.) Stir occasionally with large wooden spoon, pushing fabric down into dye, cracking more wax in the process. When color is deep enough (remember it is much lighter when dry), remove fabric, rinse in clean water, and allow to dry.

TO APPLY SECOND APPLICATION OF WAX: Melt wax again, as before. Add more wax blobs, covering different areas of the surface. Fig. 2 is a suggestion of areas to cover, but how the wax blobs land on the fabric determines the design. Keep most of the edges clear of wax. This second layer may go over the first, but it is not necessary to add wax to places already covered. Try to keep wax from building up too heavily in any one spot.

3

Turn and stuff.

PILLOW

MIX PURPLE DYE, dip fabric in cool clear water, crush, and then place in cool purple dye. Let stand for an hour or so until color has proper intensity. It should be quite dark (lighter when dry). Remove fabric, rinse in clear water, and let dry slightly.

TO REMOVE WAX: Shake, crush, scrape, and try to remove as much as possible the accumulations of wax without hurting the fabric. Then place fabric between sheets of old newspapers and press with a warm iron. Change newspapers constantly as you see the wax being absorbed. When all wax is removed, you will see the full beauty of the abstract design you have created.

4

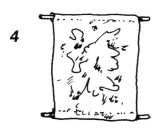

WALL HANGING

A SIMPLE REMEDY: If there is too much white, you may have been carried away and blobbed on too much wax; next time cover less of the area. It is the unwaxed areas that take the color. To remedy a design that has too much white space, mix a small amount of dye and apply with a brush to areas needing color. If you would like a third color without going through another wax step, it can be added this way also.

TO FINISH: For a scarf, sew a rolled hem all around.

5

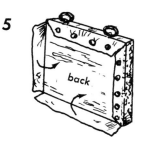

back

Tack around board.

For pillow, cut a plain piece of fabric, same size as dyed piece. Stitch around edges (right sides together), leaving part of one side open. Turn right side out, stuff, and sew closed (Fig. 3). Or the batik fabric can be sewn to one side of a purchased pillow.

For a wall decoration, roll hems on each side. Make a 1″ hem top and bottom and run a hanging rod through each hem (Fig. 4). Tack fabric around a board to hang as a wall panel or frame it (Fig. 5). Make several

See color photograph facing page 57.

panels for a screen. For screen or wall panel, spray with plastic after mounting.

TO CLEAN BATIK (after use): Dry-cleaning is preferred (this removes any traces of wax). But you can wash it in cool water.

VARIATIONS
Experiment with color combinations, such as blue over yellow, or orange with pink. Make panels of various sizes, long ones for long scarfs, large ones for hangings.

8. QUICK GIFTS BY THE DOZEN

Many of the projects in this chapter will give you a chance to use up all the odds and ends of felt, trims, and fabric scraps left over from bigger undertakings. These suggestions for making quick gifts are just springboards to your own venturesome ideas. Trims, color combinations, and designs can of course be varied to suit the materials you have at hand.

Because most of these projects are simple, you can turn them out in quantity. Set up some sort of production line and enlist the talents of the family or friends. You can make favors for a party, stocking stuffers for Christmas, or little items to fill a bargain table at a bazaar. Inexpensive bazaar items sell well if they are attractive enough to appeal to the impulse buyer. Such trinkets also enable children to purchase a gift with their own money.

When an occasion arises that calls for a little remembrance rather than a gift, one of these simple projects may be just the answer. Whether for giving or selling, all are easy to make and require very little time.

COVERED MATCHES

MATERIALS NEEDED
Book matches
Adhesive-backed vinyl and burlap, or foil gift-wrap paper
Trims such as plastic beads, gold-foil edging, etc.
Also needed: White glue

A

gold foil edging

MAKE A PATTERN on a piece of paper by opening the matchbook out flat and drawing around it. Cut pattern and fit around to make sure it is long enough. (Leave striking panel uncovered.)

CUT this size of adhesive-backed vinyl or burlap. Peel off backing and stick on. If using foil gift-wrap, cut and glue on.

B

DECORATE with whatever you have handy. For instance:

A) If you cover the matchbook with woodgrain vinyl, decorate with gold-foil edging, glued below striking panel, covering staple area. On flap, glue gold-foil oval and small foil medallion.

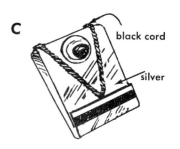

C

black cord

silver

B) On blue burlap, glue a small flat plastic flower or appliqué motifs.

C) On silver foil, glue black braid or cord. Add a surrealistic touch by gluing on a single "eye," the kind made for stuffed toys.

NAPKIN RINGS

MATERIALS NEEDED
Cardboard center roll from wax paper (foil, etc.)
Adhesive-backed vinyl, foil gift-wrap papers
Edgings, yarn, ties, etc.
White glue
Paint, latex or acrylic (color to complement trim)
Also needed: Brush (for paint)

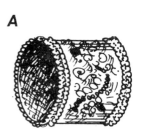

A

CUT cardboard tube into segments, each 1¾" wide, for rings. Paint inside and along cut edges.

See color photograph facing page 56.

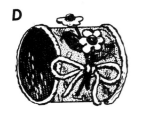

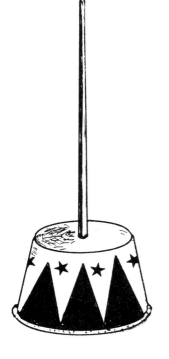

MEASURE   circumference, cut decorative paper or vinyl this length, 1¾" wide.

STICK   or glue on around the cardboard ring. Add edgings that are appropriate to background in color and texture. For instance:

A)   Cover with orange and pink foil gift-wrap, glue on woven orange yarn edging.

B)   Cover with black vinyl, strip of silver edging in middle, silver gift cord around edges.

C)   Cover with tan burlap, edge with thin orange rope or raffia.

D)   Cover with silver and blue paisley, edge with silver cord. If desired, tie a bow around a tiny artificial flower and glue on.

NOTE SPINDLE

MATERIALS NEEDED
6" or 7" knitting needle (No. 3 or 4)
Plaster of Paris
Paper or plastic cup (tapered or pointed)
1 box gummed silver stars
10" silver cord (gift-wrap)
Black adhesive-backed vinyl
3" square black felt
Spray-on varnish
Also needed: Empty bottle, coping saw, white glue

MIX   plaster of Paris (according to directions on package) in the cup. Plaster should not be more than about 2" deep in cup. Allow to stand several minutes. As it begins to thicken, hold cup (right side up) and push point of knitting needle down through the plaster and out through center of bottom of cup. The other end of the needle should be just below surface of the plaster. Set the cup on top of an empty bottle, which allows room for the needle to hang down inside, while the plaster sets. After several hours, remove and peel the cup away from the plaster. Be careful not to damage the plaster. Turn spindle over and allow to dry for several days.

TO DECORATE: Cut some triangles of black vinyl. Stick vinyl on base. Stick stars between black triangles and around base of needle. Spray varnish over base. Glue felt to bottom and trim evenly all around.

VARIATIONS

Plaster can be sanded, carved, or shaped as desired. Decorate with any motifs you choose. Or apply a coat of gesso, allow to dry thoroughly, then paint.

NATURE BOOKMARK

MATERIALS NEEDED

Dried weeds, flowers, butterflies, etc. (see Oshibana Stationery, page 48)

2½″ × 8¼″ clear, medium weight, tablecloth plastic

2½″ × 8¼″ clear adhesive-backed vinyl

Gold edging (soutache braid)

Paper

DRAW area 1⅝″ × 7½″ on paper. To plan bookmark, arrange your dried material in this rectangle. To guide you in transferring arrangement, draw a second rectangle of same size on another piece of paper.

TO ASSEMBLE: Peel backing off vinyl and lay vinyl, sticky side up, over second-drawn rectangle. Keeping within this rectangle, lay each piece exactly in place, since dried pieces cannot be shifted or picked up again. When arrangement is complete on sticky surface, lay the clear plastic (the one without adhesive) over arrangement and press down so dried material is sandwiched between the two clear pieces. Smooth out any air bubbles.

TRIM edges to make a bookmark 2¼″ × 8″. Glue on gold edging about ¼″ in from edge to frame the dried-flower arrangement.

ROCK PAPERWEIGHTS

MATERIALS NEEDED
Assortment of rounded rocks
Epoxy putty in stick form
Variety of pine cones (or acorn caps)
Raffia (optional)
Black felt pen
Also needed: Masking tape, knife (to cut cones)

CLEAN rocks and allow to dry. Place rocks against each other to see what kind of creatures they suggest.

scale

pine cone scales

ASSEMBLE: When you have decided on a good combination of rocks, mix putty according to directions. You will need very little to make the three examples shown, about ¼" slice off each stick. Place a small dab of epoxy on the body rock. Push head rock down firmly into putty. Usually it will hold. If not, prop up or tape in position while putty sets. Remove any excess putty; joining should be inconspicuous.

For caterpillar, add a third rock. After putty sets on body, small rocks can be added for ears, or feet, or whatever the sizes and shapes of your rocks suggest.

TO FINISH: When putty is hard and rocks are firmly in place, cut pine cones, using tops of cones for "hats"; use single pieces (a scale) of a large cone for wings, feet, or tails. Mix another small batch of putty and attach the pine-cone pieces to the rocks. A raffia tie can be added as a collar. With black-felt marker, draw dots for eyes and add a mouth if needed.

NET SCRUBBER

MATERIALS NEEDED

Two 5″ strips of colored nylon net (usually about 2 yds. wide)
Sewing thread in matching color
5½″ gold gift-wrap cord (or colored cord, possibly left over from
    other projects such as macramé)
Also needed: large needle

LAY two strips together.

SEW: Use double thread in the needle; knot the end. Start at end of strip (about 2½″ up from lower right corner). With a long loose running stitch, sew through both layers of net, along center line, gathering the net as you sew. When you reach the other end of the strips, fold around and sew to the starting end at knot. Pull thread as tightly as possible and pass it around center of gathered net once or twice. Sew through gathers several times to hold gathering tight. Leave needle attached.

HANGER: Fold cord in half. Place ends on sewn gathers. Using the needle and thread that is still attached, sew into and around both ends of the cord.

TO SHAPE: Pull and twist gathers where necessary to make an attractive ball shape.

VARIATIONS

To make a variegated ball, use strips of contrasting color net. Three strips will make a fuller ball.

GRASSHOPPER NOTE HOLDER

MATERIALS NEEDED
Clip clothespin
2 ice-cream sticks
2 flat toothpicks
Green, black, and white paint; varnish (spray-on)
Also needed: White glue, knife, small brush (for black and white paint)

CUT STICKS: With a knife, cut ends off one ice-cream stick, making stick the exact length of the clothespin. The cut-off ends (about ½" each) will become pieces for eyes. For legs, cut two 2" pieces of the other ice-cream stick, making angle as shown to form top angle of leg.

GLUE long stick on top of the clothespin for grasshopper's back. Glue one eye (½" end of stick) on one side. Glue toothpick and angled-stick leg on side as shown. Break toothpick to proper length. Add glue at top joining. Allow to dry. Glue the stick and toothpick leg pieces to *bottom* section of clothespin only. Otherwise, it cannot be opened to hold notes. Turn over and glue other eye and leg pieces to other side. Allow glue to dry.

TO DECORATE: Drip glue drops to make little lumps. Space four or five drops along the back of the grasshopper. Allow to dry. Lay on side, drip four drops on leg, drip one large drop on for eye. When dry, turn over and repeat on other side. Allow to dry thoroughly.

SPRAY-PAINT a bright green (fluorescent, if desired). Paint dabs of white and black on eyes.

TO FINISH: Spray varnish over entire piece.

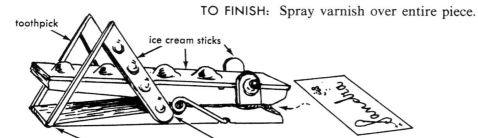

toothpick

ice cream sticks

Glue legs here only.

9. GIFTS TO TICKLE THE PALATE

For a holiday or hostess present, nothing is more welcomed by the whole family than a gift of food. Culinary creations are always a sellout at fund-raising events. Here are some new, exciting. recipes from Betty Crocker. All are kitchen-tested and selected with imagination and good taste.

Edible gifts are even more fun when they are attractively displayed and packaged. In the second part of Chapter 10, you will find specific suggestions for containers as well as wraps to enhance food, either for giving or fund-raising.

Try a few of these festive recipes for your own family. Then the next time an occasion arises or items are needed for a bazaar, you'll be all set with gift packages of your favorite foods. See color photograph facing page 152.

QUICK BUTTERMILK BREAD

2 packages active dry yeast
1½ cups warm water (105 to 115°)
2½ cups buttermilk
9 to 10 cups all-purpose flour*
½ cup shortening
¼ cup sugar
1 tablespoon plus 1 teaspoon baking powder
1 tablespoon plus 1 teaspoon salt
Soft butter or margarine

Grease 2 loaf pans, 9″ × 5″ × 3″. Dissolve yeast in warm water in large mixer bowl. Add buttermilk, 5 cups of the flour, the shortening, sugar, baking powder, and salt. Blend 1 minute on low speed, scraping side and bottom of bowl. Beat 4 minutes on medium speed. Stir in remaining 4 to 5 cups flour. (Dough should remain soft and slightly sticky.) Divide dough in half; knead each half 5 minutes or about 200 turns on generously floured board. Roll each half into rectangle, 18″ × 9″. Roll up from short side as for jelly roll. With side of hand, press each end to seal. Fold ends under loaf. Place seam side down in pan. Brush loaves lightly with butter. Let rise in warm place until double, about 1 hour. (Dough in center should come about 2″ above pans.)

Heat oven to 425°. Oven rack should be in lowest position or bread will brown too quickly. Bake loaves *30 to 35 minutes.* Remove from pans and brush with butter; cool on wire racks.
2 loaves.
* *If using self-rising flour, omit baking powder and salt.*

VARIATIONS

HERB BREAD

Add 1 tablespoon plus 1 teaspoon caraway seed, 1 teaspoon crumbled leaf sage, and 1 teaspoon nutmeg to yeast-water mixture.

GARLIC BREAD

Add 1½ teaspoons garlic powder to yeast-water mixture.

CHEESE BREAD

Omit shortening. Stir in 2 cups shredded sharp natural Cheddar cheese with second addition of flour.

CANDIED FRUIT SWIRL

Spread each rectangle with mixture of 1 cup chopped candied fruit, 2 tablespoons vanilla, and 1 teaspoon rum extract.

TO FREEZE QUICK BUTTERMILK BREAD: Cool to room temperature after baking. (Do not freeze unbaked dough.) Wrap in plastic bags or aluminum foil; freeze immediately. Store frozen breads up to 12 months. To thaw, let stand at room temperature 2 to 3 hours in wrapping.

TOASTED SESAME-SEED TOFFEE

1 cup sugar
1 cup butter
1 cup toasted sesame seed

In a large skillet, heat sugar and butter to boiling, stirring constantly. Cook and stir over medium heat until mixture caramelizes (becomes light brown and thickened), about 10 minutes. Remove from heat; stir in seed. Turn onto ungreased baking sheet; spread ¼ inch thick. Cool; break into pieces. (Store at room temperature.)

If toffee is to be sold at a bazaar, package it in small plastic bags, overwrap with colorful tissue paper, and tie with bright yarn.

About 1 pound.

Note: To toast sesame seed, heat oven to 350°. Spread seed in baking pan; toast, stirring frequently, until pale golden color, *about 10 minutes.*

NO-COOK DIVINITY

1 package (7.2 ounces) fluffy white frosting mix
$^1/_3$ cup light corn syrup
1 teaspoon vanilla
½ cup boiling water
1 package (16 ounces) confectioners' sugar
1 cup chopped nuts

Combine frosting mix (dry), corn syrup, vanilla, and boiling water in small mixer bowl. Beat on highest speed until stiff peaks form, about 5 minutes. Transfer to large mixer bowl. On low speed or by hand, gradually blend in sugar; stir in nuts.

Drop mixture by teaspoonfuls onto waxed paper. When outside of candy feels firm, turn over and allow to dry at least 12 hours. Store candy in airtight container.

5 to 6 dozen candies.

VARIATIONS
SPANISH CRUNCH

Substitute dark corn syrup for the light, and salted Spanish peanuts for the chopped nuts.

CANDIED CHERRY DELIGHTS

Substitute 1 teaspoon almond extract for the vanilla and 1 cup chopped candied cherries for the nuts. If desired, tint with few drops red food color.

PEPPY MINTS

Substitute ½ teaspoon peppermint extract for the vanilla and 1 cup crushed peppermint candy for the nuts. If desired, tint with few drops green food color.

RIBBON FUDGE

2 tablespoons butter or margarine
¼ cup plus 2 teaspoons milk
1 package (15.4 ounces) chocolate fudge frosting mix
½ cup chopped nuts
2 tablespoons butter or margarine
¼ cup milk
1 package (15.4 ounces) creamy white frosting mix
½ cup chopped nuts

CHOCOLATE LAYER: Line bottom of square pan, 8″ × 8″ × 2″, with aluminum foil, leaving 1″ of foil at opposite sides. In medium saucepan, heat 2 tablespoons butter in ¼ cup plus 2 teaspoons milk over low heat until butter melts and mixture *just* begins to simmer. Remove from heat; stir in chocolate fudge frosting mix (dry). Heat over low heat, stirring constantly with rubber scraper, until smooth and glossy, 1 to 2 minutes. *Do not overcook.* Remove from heat; stir in ½ cup nuts. Spread in pan.

WHITE LAYER: Repeat with remaining 2 tablespoons butter, ¼ cup milk, the white frosting mix, and nuts. Spread over chocolate in pan, making 2 layers. Chill until firm. Lift candy out; cut into 1″ squares.

64 squares.

DELUXE HOLIDAY FRUITCAKE

1 package (14 ounces) date bar mix
²/₃ cup hot water
3 eggs
2 tablespoons light molasses
¼ cup all-purpose flour
¾ teaspoon baking powder
1 teaspoon cinnamon
¼ teaspoon nutmeg
¼ teaspoon allspice
1 cup whole blanched almonds
1 cup cut-up candied pineapple
1 cup whole candied red cherries

Heat oven to 325°. Grease and flour loaf pan, 9″ × 5″ × 3″. In large bowl, combine date filling from date bar mix and hot water. Blend in crumbly mix from date bar mix, eggs, molasses, flour, baking powder, and spices. Stir in nuts and fruits. Spread mixture evenly in pan. Bake *about 1 hour 20 minutes* or until wooden pick inserted in center comes out clean. Cool; wrap well. Refrigerate or freeze.

TO FREEZE DELUXE HOLIDAY FRUITCAKE: Cool to room temperature after baking. (Do not freeze unbaked batter.) Place on cardboard; wrap in plastic wrap or aluminum foil. Store frozen fruitcake up to 6 months. To thaw, let stand at room temperature 1 hour in wrapping.

Note: Fruitcake loaf can be sliced in half or in thirds and wrapped in clear plastic wrap to show off large candied fruits.

"Hot" Port Wine Jelly (page 157); Nutty Caramel Corn (page 157); Marzipan Cookies (page 155); Quick Buttermilk Bread (page 148); Frosted Ham-Cheese Ball (page 153)

Food and Gift Wraps (page 158)

FROSTED HAM-CHEESE BALL

  3 cans (4½ ounces each) deviled ham
  1 teaspoon dry mustard
  ⅛ teaspoon ginger
  3 packages (8 ounces each) cream cheese, softened
  2 tablespoons snipped chives
  ½ cup grated Parmesan cheese

Mix deviled ham, mustard, and ginger. Chill in freezer until firm, about 1 hour. Mix cream cheese and chives.

Shape chilled ham mixture into ball; cover evenly with cream cheese mixture. Cover with plastic wrap; refrigerate until firm, about 3 hours.

Sprinkle Parmesan cheese on sheet of waxed paper. Place cheese ball in center and gently press Parmesan cheese on ball. (Cheese ball can be covered with plastic wrap and refrigerated up to 5 days.)

Decorate like a tree ornament with slices of stuffed olives, pimiento strips, and snipped parsley. Serve with small crackers.

About 24 servings.

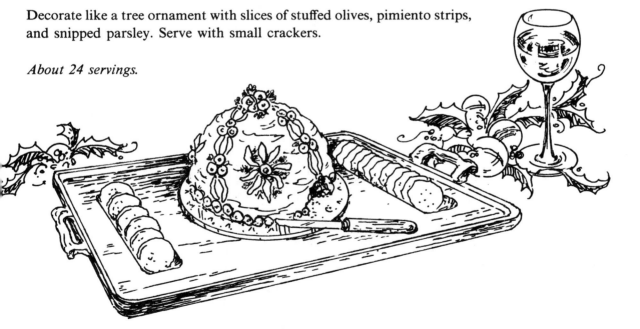

BONBON COOKIES

½ cup butter or margarine, softened
¾ cup confectioners' sugar
1 tablespoon vanilla
Food color, if desired
1½ cups all-purpose flour*
⅛ teaspoon salt
Dates, nuts, semisweet chocolate pieces, and candied or maraschino
    cherries
Icing (below)

Heat oven to 350°. Mix thoroughly butter, sugar, vanilla, and few drops
food color. Work in flour and salt until dough holds together. (If dough
is dry, mix in 1 to 2 tablespoons light cream or half-and-half.)

Mold dough by tablespoonfuls around date, nut, chocolate piece, or
cherry. Place cookies about 1″ apart on ungreased baking sheet. Bake *12
to 15 minutes* or until set but not brown.

Cool; dip tops of cookies into icing. If desired, decorate each with coconut,
nuts, colored sugar, chocolate pieces, or chocolate shot.

20 to 25 cookies.

* *Do not use self-rising flour in this recipe.*

ICING: Mix 1 cup confectioners' sugar, 2½ tablespoons light cream
or 1½ tablespoons milk, and 1 teaspoon vanilla until smooth. If desired,
stir in few drops food color. For a chocolate icing, increase light cream
to 3 tablespoons or milk to 2 tablespoons and stir in 1 ounce melted
unsweetened chocolate (cool).

MARZIPAN COOKIES

1 cup butter or margarine, softened
½ cup sugar
2½ cups all-purpose flour*
½ to 1 teaspoon almond extract
Food color

Cream butter and sugar. Stir in flour and almond extract until mixture looks like meal. Divide into 3 equal parts. Color and make some of the shapes as directed below. Place cookies on ungreased baking sheet; chill ½ hour.

Heat oven to 300°. Bake *30 minutes* or until set but not brown.

About 4 dozen cookies.

* *Do not use self-rising flour in this recipe.*

STRAWBERRIES: Mix red food color into 1 part of the dough. Shape dough into small balls; form each into heart shape (about ¾ inch high). For texture, prick shapes with blunt end of wooden pick. Roll each in red sugar. Insert small piece of green-colored wooden pick or green dough in top of each for stem.

BANANAS: Mix yellow food color into 1 part of the dough. Shape dough into 3″ rolls, tapering ends to resemble a banana. Flatten tops slightly to show planes of banana and curve each slightly. Paint on characteristic markings with mixture of red, yellow, and blue food color diluted with water.

ORANGES: Mix red and yellow food color into 1 part of the dough. Shape dough into small balls. Insert whole clove in each for blossom end. For peel texture, prick balls with blunt end of wooden pick.

QUICK STRAWBERRY PRESERVES

2 packages (10 ounces each) frozen sliced strawberries, partially thawed
1 tablespoon lemon juice
2 tablespoons powdered fruit pectin
2 cups sugar

Prepare glasses (see note). In covered saucepan, cook strawberries and lemon juice over high heat 2 minutes. Stir in pectin; heat to rolling boil, stirring constantly. Boil and stir 1 minute. Add sugar; heat to rolling boil, stirring constantly. Boil and stir 1 minute. Remove from heat; immediately skim off foam. Fill glasses and seal with paraffin. (Or cover preserves and store in refrigerator up to 2 months.)

Note: To prepare glasses, place clean jelly glasses in pan with folded cloth on bottom. Cover with hot, not boiling, water and heat to boiling. Boil gently 15 minutes; keep glasses in hot water until ready to use. When ready to fill, remove glasses from water and drain.

Four 6-ounce glasses.

SPICY SUGARED NUTS

1 egg white or 2 tablespoons egg white
4 cups pecans or walnuts
½ cup sugar
2 tablespoons cinnamon

Heat oven to 300°. In bowl, mix egg white and nuts, stirring until nuts are coated and sticky.

Mix sugar and cinnamon; sprinkle over nuts, stirring until sugar mixture completely coats nuts. Spread on ungreased baking sheet. Bake *30 minutes.*

About 4 cups nuts.

"HOT" PORT WINE JELLY

    1 tablespoon crushed dried hot peppers
    2 cups red port wine
    3 cups sugar
    1 teaspoon yellow food color
    ¾ teaspoon red food color
    ½ bottle (6-ounce size) liquid pectin

Stir peppers into wine. Cover and let stand at least 3 hours.

Prepare glasses (see note, opposite page). Strain wine into saucepan; stir in sugar and food colors. Heat over low heat, stirring constantly, until sugar is dissolved, about 5 minutes. Remove from heat; immediately stir in pectin. Skim off foam. Fill glasses and seal with paraffin.

Four or five 8-ounce glasses.

NUTTY CARAMEL CORN

    12 cups popped corn
    3 cups walnut halves, pecan halves
      and/or unblanched whole almonds
    1 cup brown sugar (packed)
    ½ cup butter or margarine
    ¼ cup light corn syrup
    ½ teaspoon salt
    ½ teaspoon soda

Heat oven to 200°. Divide popped corn and nuts between 2 ungreased oblong pans, 13″ × 9″ × 2″. Heat sugar, butter, corn syrup, and salt, stirring occasionally, until bubbly around edges. Continue cooking over medium heat 5 minutes.

Remove from heat; stir in soda until foamy. Pour over popped corn and nuts, stirring until well coated. Bake uncovered *1 hour,* stirring every 15 minutes.

10. WRAPPING THINGS UP

After long, patient hours of creating the perfect present, it would be a pity not to take a little extra thought and time to wrap it imaginatively. Any gift-giving occasion is heightened by suspense as the tantalizing wrapping that conceals its mysterious contents is admired. Anticipation adds to the festivities, and a gaily wrapped present can make any day a holiday.

Papers, ribbons, boxes, decorations, trims, wrapping unusual shapes — all phases of preparing packages will be briefly discussed here to help you cope with any gift-wrap problem. Since there are some special tricks in wrapping food packages, these will be reserved for the second part of this chapter.

The assortment of gift-wrap materials in stationery, variety, department, and greeting-card stores becomes more exciting every year. Your choice depends on your budget, your taste, the occasion, and the shape of the package you want to wrap. If you have a large selection of materials on hand, inventiveness becomes easier. And when all elements fuse together, a package can become a work of art. See color photograph facing page 153.

GIFT WRAPPING

PAPER

Many types of gift wrap papers are available in a wide range of prices and weights. Choose plain colors or attractive patterns which have been designed for specific gift occasions. Tissue paper, plain or variegated (Madras), is less expensive, but it makes a very pretty package wrap.

Flocks and tinseled papers are more difficult to handle, but they are worth the effort for an especially elegant gift. If tape doesn't hold the ends closed, use glue.

Foils are very versatile and they come in many weights and designs, either printed or embossed. If you plan to add decorations, trims, or an especially fancy ribbon to your package, choose a plain color foil.

ORIGINAL WRAPS

Your imagination will lead you to other sources. Use fabrics, printed paper toweling, colored shelf paper. A huge present may call for a printed paper tablecloth; a tiny one, a scrap of gold lamé. Think about the paper you have around the house. Enlist leftover wallpapers, vinyl, colorful posters, printed paper guest towels or napkins, road maps. Even comic sheets or appropriate sections of the newspaper make effective wrapping with colorful ribbon or trim. Almost anything flexible can become an unusual gift-wrap.

HAND-DECORATED PAPER

To supply a personal touch for a special gift, make your own gift-wrap. Simple techniques used in schools can be adapted for this purpose. A child's letter-stamp set, or other rubber stamps, and a good stamp pad (from stationery shop), can be used for initials, names, or seasonal messages. Household items, such as a rubber sink stopper, pencil eraser, cork stopper, etc., pressed on the stamp pad, can create designs when repeated across the paper. Stamps, in the shape of stars and other decorative designs, are available in toy or stationery stores. When these designs are stamped in groups, or overlapping, they form an effective overall pattern. Or motifs can be stenciled (see page 53).

ink pad

sink stoppe

However, if you have to print large areas of wrapping paper, a roller is most efficient.

MATERIALS NEEDED
Mailing tube (large enough diameter to fit over a rolling pin)
Rolling pin
String or twine
Scrap of thick fabric or art foam
Paper
Latex paint
Colored tissue, wrapping paper (or other large piece of plain wrapping paper)
Fabric glue
Also needed: Old cooky sheet, ice-cream stick (or spatula), mat knife, old newspapers, old rag

TO MAKE ROLLER: Cut the mailing tube so it is long enough to cover the roller part of the rolling pin, but allow handles to be exposed.

PLAN your design on paper (Fig. 1). Draw the design, name, or message with a soft pencil. Then place the paper face down against the tube. Trace on the back of the paper over the lines drawn, to transfer a reverse drawing onto the tube.

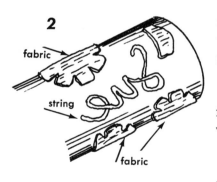

CUT the shapes out of fabric, following the paper pattern. Use a fabric with some thickness and texture (such as corduroy) or art foam, which is 1/8" thick.

ATTACH SHAPES   to the tube with fabric glue. Lay glue over the line design and glue string or twine along the shape drawn (Fig. 2). Allow glue to dry thoroughly. Slide the tube onto the rolling pin (Fig. 3).

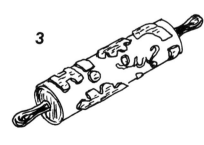

TO PAINT: Spread newspaper, then paper to be used, on a flat surface. Place a little latex paint on an old cooky sheet. With a stick or spatula, spread out the paint, making a thin layer on the cooky sheet. Keep turning the roller in the paint and roll onto old newspaper. The first few times will probably produce blobs. Wipe off any accumulation of paint on the roller. When the pattern appears clear and neat on the newspaper, then roll into the paint and roll across the paper to be used for wrapping. Clean up tools. Allow printed designs on the paper to dry.

If you wish to vary this, plan and glue new shapes to another piece of the tube and repeat, using a different color.

VARIATIONS

For more delicate gradation of textures, use water-based ink made for block printing (available in art stores). With a roller made for this purpose, spread ink on heavy glass or on old cooky sheet. This ink comes in brighter colors than the latex, but it takes much longer to dry.

Any combination of means for adding designs can be used to create handmade gift-wrap. Use the roller to establish a simple grid or pattern. Stencil or add stamped motifs between these areas (Fig. 4). Look at well-designed gift-wraps in the stores for pattern and color ideas. Personalize your designs with initials or names.

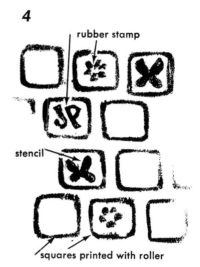

4

rubber stamp

stencil

squares printed with roller

HOW TO WRAP A BOX

IN PAPER

Once you have chosen your paper, you can wrap the box containing your gift. It's as simple as 1-2-3.

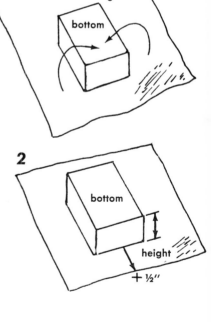

1

paper
wrong side

bottom

2

bottom

height

+ ½"

MATERIALS NEEDED
Box
Paper
Transparent tape

TO CUT PAPER: Lay box on paper, loosely fold around, and allow for overlap (Fig. 1). This determines the width of the paper. Cut width. Then measure height of box, add about ½" (Fig. 2), and cut this length.

TO WRAP: Wrap width around box. Fold under uneven edge about ¼" (Fig. 3), overlap, and tape.

FOR ENDS: Fold down one end (Fig. 4). Fold in the triangular shape

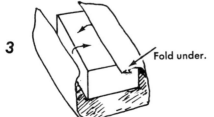

3

Fold under.

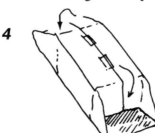

4

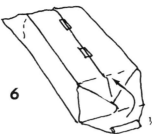

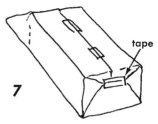

5 Fold in.

6 ½" fold (approx.)

7 tape

at each corner (Fig. 5). Fold up the flap. Fold under edge of the flap about ½" (Fig. 6). Tape flap to box (Fig. 7). Repeat on other end.

Package is now ready for ribbon, trim, and tag.

IN PLASTIC

Sometimes the most unlikely materials can be turned into gift-wraps. Many home products are packaged in plastic wraps, often with colorful designs. Some stores sell plastic shopping bags or give them to customers with a purchase. Trash and leaf bags come in various sizes and colors. From these sources a collage-type gift-wrap can be created.

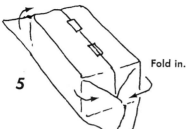

gold cord

sequins glued on dots

Black plastic, gold dots (from a bookstore bag).

MATERIALS NEEDED
Plastic bags (interesting colors and designs)
Rubber cement
Transparent tape
Sequins or other trims (optional)
Also needed (optional): Warm iron, brown wrapping paper

SELECT PLASTIC MATERIAL: If it is to be used for a huge package, a leaf bag is good. For smaller packages, a section of a shopping bag or bread wrapper may be usable. Cut off any printed message.

If wrapper is wrinkled or crushed, it may need smoothing. Place plastic between two sheets of brown wrapping paper. With iron set at lowest temperature, go over wrapping paper gently to flatten the plastic beneath. Never place iron near the plastic itself, since plastic is very sensitive to heat and would melt onto the iron.

Plastic bag from a dessert food product.

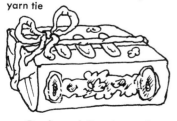

yarn tie

FOLD plastic around the package, tape closed as you would any gift-wrap.

TO DECORATE: Cover the areas you plan to embellish with rubber cement. Cut ornaments from other wraps: stars, from bread wrappers; flowers, or geometric shapes of contrasting colors, from other bags. Apply

Ovals and florals cut from another food bag.

rubber cement to back of each piece you plan to add. When cement is dry, attach to box, making interesting arrangements. Rub off any excess cement with your fingers.

ADD TRIMS: Glue on sequins, snowflakes, stars, etc. Add ribbon, stick on a bow. A few examples are shown here.

Wrapped in huge red shopping bag (or leaf bag).

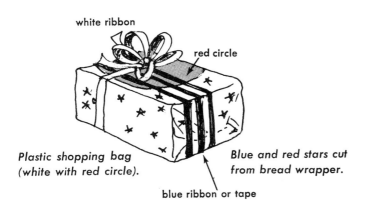

white ribbon

red circle

Plastic shopping bag (white with red circle).

Blue and red stars cut from bread wrapper.

blue ribbon or tape

Santa cut from shopping bag.

RIBBONS AND BOWS

Metallic cords, yarn ties, ribbons of all kinds, and pre-made bows are sold for gift wrapping. But that is just the beginning. For instance, you might use hair ties made of plastic, leather, or bulky yarn. From the notions counter, you might adapt all kinds of trims, especially braids (soutache, middy, featherloop braid, gimp, rickrack, etc.). Some gold braids have adhesive backing for special effects. Tie velvet tubing or strung sequins on a special tiny package.

Other interesting ties include plastic chains, plastic beads on a string, tinsel garlands (used for decorating Christmas trees), hemp or sisal cord, bulky string, nylon twine, etc. Those lacking color may be dipped in fabric dye. Most take color readily.

When you wrap a package for mailing, avoid bows or other crushable ornaments. Sticky-backed ribbon can be folded to resemble a tailored bow. Yarn ties, glitter, pipe cleaners, gift cords all pack well.

There are several basic ways to tie a ribbon or cord around a package.

MATERIALS NEEDED
Ribbon or cord
Wrapped package

Bows for mailing

cord

adhesive-backed ribbon

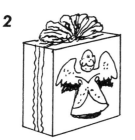

TIE lengthwise or crosswise or both. Slide ribbon or cord slightly to left side and create interesting space proportions (Fig. 1). A tie directly across the middle is uninteresting.

TIE around narrow side, adding decoration on broad side (Fig. 2).

TO MAKE A DIAGONAL TIE: Hold end of ribbon on upper left corner. Unroll ribbon, going down under the lower left corner, *up* over lower right corner (Fig. 3). Go down under upper right corner and up to meet the point where you are holding the starting end (Fig. 4). Cut off ribbon, allowing enough extra to tie. If you keep sufficient tension on the ribbon, this works easily. Tie knot and add a bow.

This is especially effective if you plan a decorative unit for the center (Fig. 5) or if tag is large and colorful.

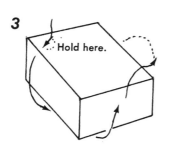

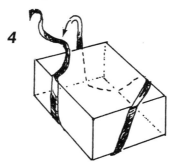

TAGS AND ENCLOSURE CARDS

Enclosure cards and tags should be considered part of an attractive gift-wrap. There are many tags and cards available or you can make your own.

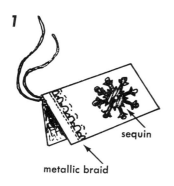

MATERIALS NEEDED
Gold card (back of a greeting card)
Old greeting cards
White paper, thin card (optional)
Gift-wrap
Sequins or braid
Thin cord or string (for tags)
Small envelopes (for enclosure card)
Also needed: White glue, awl or paper punch

FOLDED TAGS: Cut a piece of gold card about 2½" × 3". Fold in half. If some printing shows inside, cut a piece of white paper 1½" × 2½". Paste inside card.

Glue trims to card (Fig. 1), or cut motifs from seasonal cards and glue on. Punch a small hole in upper left inside corner with an awl or punch. Tie on string.

Small motifs from gift-wrap paper also make good tags. Glue motif to white card, fold, and add tie.

FLAT TAGS: Select appropriate size design from an old greeting card or mount a motif from gift-wrap. Trim around the decorative piece (Fig. 2). Add cord decorations along edges if desired. Punch hole in top, add cord.

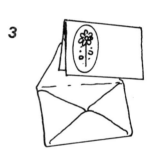

2

ENCLOSURE CARDS: Purchase small envelopes and make cards to fit. Cut a flat rectangle to proper size or make double-size card and fold over (Fig. 3). A plain white card is usually most appropriate. Decorations like the ones used on the tags can be added.

Oshibana flowers make treasured enclosure cards (see page 48).

3

PACKAGE DECORATIONS

After a gift has been handsomely wrapped with appropriate paper and tied with a perky bow, it certainly is ready to present. But sometimes you may want to add an extra decorative note to make the packaging more personal.

When you plan such a decoration, it's best to wrap the gift in a plain-color paper or foil. Even a ribbon or bow may not be necessary.

An appropriate picture from an old greeting card makes an easy, inexpensive trim. Cut off back, trim to size, and fasten to the box with glue or double-stick tape. Gold-foil photo-mount corners add extra elegance.

Purchased trims should be jaunty and vivid, yet need not be costly. Greeting-card and party-supply shops offer all sorts of items you can convert to trims. Choose from party favors, plastic charms, cardboard and paper party decorations, to add whimsy, charm, and glamour to gifts. Here are three ideas for using party supplies as package trims.

MATERIALS NEEDED

Gift package (wrapped in plain paper)
Paper fan or coasters or cardboard ashtrays
Ribbon and bow
Sequins or trims
Tape and white glue

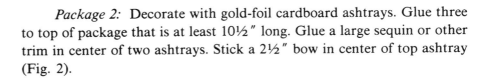

Package 1: Open out paper fan, and tape or glue to top of package. Tie ribbon around corners to help hold fan in place (Fig. 1). Tie on a tag reading: "To —— from one of your fans."

Package 2: Decorate with gold-foil cardboard ashtrays. Glue three to top of package that is at least 10½ " long. Glue a large sequin or other trim in center of two ashtrays. Stick a 2½ " bow in center of top ashtray (Fig. 2).

Package 3: On a fairly large-size package, scatter colorful paper coasters in a pleasing arrangement. Glue down (or attach with double-stick tape). Tie on ribbon, add a bow (Fig. 3).

A tag or enclosure card can be made to match. Fold a piece of paper in half and glue a coaster on top. Trim to fit the coaster (Fig. 4). Write message inside. If you use it as a tag, add a cord and attach to bow.

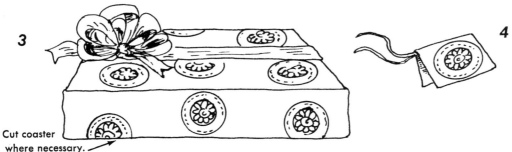

Cut coaster where necessary.

"HINT" PACKAGE TRIMS

Trims can add to the fun by giving clues to the identity of the gift. To make a "hint" wrapping, explore the section of your variety store that relates to the gift (cosmetic, kitchen, sewing, or whatever). Tucked away in that department are usually some inexpensive trinkets that would be appropriate as a gift "topper." Or check in the toy department for small plastic replicas of adult items. Glue or tie on the "hint" trinket. Here are a few suggestions for a kitchen-shower gift or a housewarming present:

MATERIALS NEEDED
Set of plastic measuring spoons, wooden salad servers, or plastic
    utensils
Rubber cement or transparent tape
Recipe card
Plain-wrapped gift
Ribbon and bow

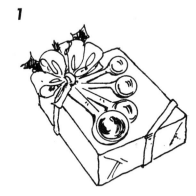

Package 1: For a kitchen gift, fan out spoon set and lay on package
to determine the best arrangement. Add a dab of rubber cement to bowl
of spoon and a dab on each place where spoons will attach to package.
When cement is dry, stick spoons on box or tape in place. (Rubber cement
can later be rubbed off so the recipient can use the spoons.) Tie a ribbon
around package through loop in spoons (Fig. 1) and add bow.

Package 2: Rubber-cement a recipe card (with a favorite recipe
written on it). Cement spoon and fork in place or tape on. Tie a ribbon
around, add bow.

VARIATIONS
Here are a few ideas for other gifts, but browsing in a store will give you
many more.

SEWING OR CLOTHING GIFT: Tie package with tape measure,
decorative braid, or strung sequins, adding on pincushion, child's scissors,
or buttons.

GARDEN OR HOUSEWARMING GIFT: Glue on seed packets, toy
tools, garden gloves, artificial flowers.

WOMAN'S PERSONAL GIFT: Tie on sample-size perfume, sachet,
hair bow, clip, or purse mirror.

MAN'S SHOP GIFT: Glue on nails, screws or washers, a "fan" of
sandpaper sheets, or toy tools.
These ideas are just to get you started. Whatever the nature of the gift,
you can probably think up a "hint" to decorate it or an extra little token
to highlight the occasion.

HOW TO COVER A BOX

New gift boxes can be expensive, but old boxes are easily re-covered. Use gift-wrap paper to refresh a dingy one. (Or make an old box durable and new-looking by covering it with a leftover piece of adhesive-backed vinyl.)

All gift boxes should look sparkling new.

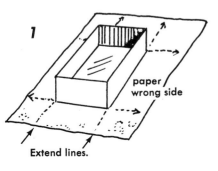

1

paper
wrong side

Extend lines.

MATERIALS NEEDED
(for paper covering)
Old gift box
Ribbon
Gift-wrap paper (fairly sturdy)
Also Needed: Pencil, ruler, rubber cement or white glue

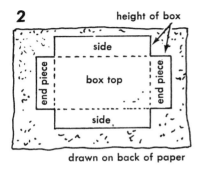

2

height of box

side

end piece   box top   end piece

side

drawn on back of paper

COVER TOP of box separately from the bottom. To plan size and shape before cutting paper, lay paper down, wrong side up. Turn top of box over and lay in center of paper (Fig. 1). Draw around box and extend the four lines. Set top aside. Measure height of box, and mark this on the paper for side pieces (Fig. 2). For flaps to fold around (to make neater corners), add ½″ extra on both sides of end pieces (Fig. 3). Taper flaps as shown.

This size will trim along edges of the box, but if a fold-over to inside is needed, add ¾″ along sides and end pieces (Fig. 4).

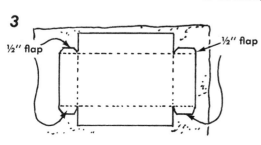

3

½″ flap   ½″ flap

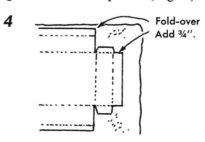

4

Fold-over
Add ¾″.

CUT SHAPE out of paper.

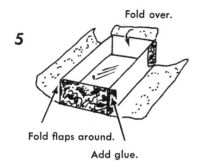

5

Fold over.

Fold flaps around.
Add glue.

TO ATTACH PAPER: Cover box surface and paper surface separately with rubber cement. Allow to dry.

SET BOX on paper in position. Fold up ends, stick on (Fig. 5). Add rubber cement over flaps. Fold up sides (Fig. 6). Trim edges even with box or turn fold-over to inside of cover. Rub off any excess rubber cement.

Thinned white glue may be used instead of rubber cement.

Repeat the process to cover the bottom section of the box (if necessary).

Now that the box is attractively covered, just tie with ribbon and trim if desired. There is no need for further wrapping.

6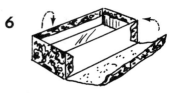

VARIATIONS

Adhesive-backed vinyl is attached in the same manner. Draw lines on backing paper. Cut out, peel off backing, and attach.

Boxes can also be covered with left-over pieces of fabric. Using fabric glue, attach along edges, sides, and joinings.

Some objects are fairly flat and square so they hardly need a box, yet one side needs protection (such as the owl plaque, page 21). In such cases there is no need for a box. Cut two pieces of corrugated cardboard of size needed to cover. Tape one to top and one to bottom (Fig. 7). Gift-wrap like any square package.

7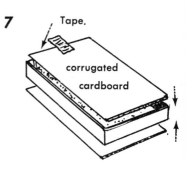

HOW TO WRAP ROUND CONTAINERS

Round objects are not difficult to wrap and make attractive packages to contrast with all the square ones.

MATERIALS NEEDED
Round can (or box)
Paper
Transparent tape
Glue
Bow or tie
Metallic cord trims (optional)

1

TAPE paper around. Extra paper on each side should measure slightly more than the dimension of the can's radius. Fold this extra paper under on bottom, as though making pleats (Fig. 1). Hold as you overlap each pleat. Then tape to hold.

FOR TOP of can, repeat process. Then cut a circle of paper slightly smaller than diameter of can. Glue circle over pleating or fasten pleats down with red or gold notary seal. Glue cord around edge of circle, if desired.

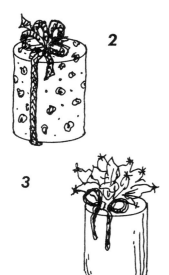

STICK on a pre-made bow or tie a ribbon around first (Fig. 2). Tape ribbon underneath bow, if necessary, to prevent slipping.

AN ALTERNATE TOP leaves paper sticking up. In this instance, allow 4″ to 6″ plus the radius of can. Bunch paper together, folding in as you gather. This creates a frill, blossoming out at the top. Tie with cord, pipe cleaner or yarn (Fig. 3). This paper frill can be cut into interesting shapes, if you wish. Stick paper stars on tips, or dream up other fanciful decorations.

TUBES

Long skinny objects can be placed inside tubes. There are usually many throw-away tubes around the house from foil, plastic wrap, mailers, etc. Table-salt boxes are basically large, round tubes (Fig. 1). After removing tops, you can place two boxes together to make a larger tube shape. Place gift inside, tape boxes together, and wrap.

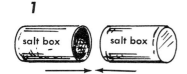

MATERIALS NEEDED
Tube
Plain paper (optional)
Gift-wrap paper, or tissue
Yarn or ribbon
Decorative motif
Transparent tape
White glue (optional)

TO PREPARE: Cut tube proper length to accommodate gift. If there is printing on tube, paste plain paper around tube to cover.

TO WRAP: Use gift paper that is not too heavy or stiff. Cut the decorative paper or tissue 6″ (or more) longer than the length of tube and wide enough to go around and overlap. Roll around tube and tape. Gather end and tie a bow of yarn or narrow ribbon to hold. Repeat on other end (Fig. 2).

TO DECORATE: Stick on a foil motif, glue on a picture (from a card), or add a package decoration.

BOTTLES

Wrapping a bottle is a similar procedure.

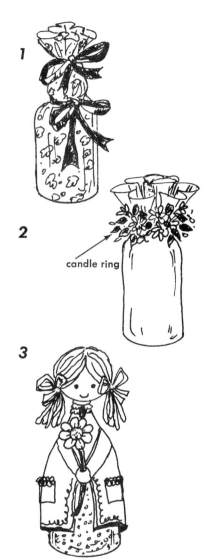

MATERIALS NEEDED
Bottle
Paper, tissue (or foil)
Yarn or cord tie
Candle ring (optional)
Transparent tape

TAPE   paper around lower portion of the bottle. If using tissue, crush it around bottle with extra paper flared out on top. Tie. For bottom, fold in (as for round can) and tape. You can crush in again at proper spot on bottle to accentuate its shape (Fig. 1). Tie.

candle ring

DECORATE   as you choose. For instance, after bottle is wrapped with tissue, tie top. Then slip a candle ring of artificial fruit or flowers over tissue onto top of bottle. Tape in place (Fig. 2). Besides being decorative, this ring can be used again by the gift's recipient.

VARIATIONS
If you wish to hide the bottle shape, wrap bottle in flexible corrugated cardboard, cut to height of bottle. Tape. Stuff tissue inside cardboard to protect the top of the bottle. Then wrap, with flare tie at top.

More ambitious craftsmen can use bottle shapes to create imaginative figures. Hollow out a foam ball sufficiently to fit over neck of bottle. Use this as a head (Fig. 3). Add yarn "hair" and facial features by gluing on fabrics, trims, and tiny accessories.

BAGS

A very irregularly shaped gift can be wrapped effectively in a bag. Ordinary brown paper bags can be gaily decorated. Cut bright-colored papers (or scraps of gift-wrap) into bold shapes. Glue to bag with rubber cement or thinned white glue. Gather top and tie with yarn or cord. Or fold down the top and fasten with a large seal.

Fabric bags are both attractive and reusable. Scraps of all kinds can be used, but samples of your tie dyeing or batik make especially striking ones.

MATERIALS NEEDED
Fabric (felt, bonded fabrics, sturdy cottons, burlaps, vinyls, uphol-
  stery fabric, etc.)
Cord, yarn, or ribbon
Also needed: Tape measure, cardboard (optional)

MEASURE   size of gift's base to make a bag that will fit. This determines size needed for base piece of fabric. Make it generous and add
¼″ all around.

FOR BODY   of bag, figure height of gift, then add 2½″. To determine
the other measurements for the body piece, add up dimensions of all four
sides of base piece (Fig. 1). Cut base and body pieces out of fabric. Pin
base to body piece.

height

base piece

1

SEW   along base (with base and body pieces wrong side out), making
¼″ seam (Fig. 2). When you come to a corner, pick up the presser foot
and adjust the fabric to sew along the next edge of base. Continue around
until all four edges of base are sewn to bag. Sew up side seam where it
meets at corner. Trim seams even to ¼″.

TO FINISH TOP: Make a channel for drawstring. Fold down 1¼″
(on wrong side) and sew edge. Sew another row of stitching ¼″ above this
(Fig. 3).

TURN   bag right side out. Cut small slit in channel in front of bag.

TO MAKE DRAWSTRING: Attach a safety pin to the end of a piece
of cord, yarn, or ribbon, pull it through the channel starting at slit, leaving
ends long enough to tie.

FOR A FIRMER BASE,   cut a piece of cardboard to fit base. Slip down
inside bag.

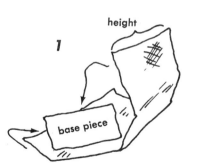

2

Sew ¼″ seam.

wrong side

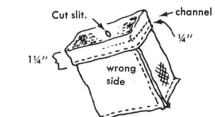

3

Cut slit.   channel

1¼″   ¼″

wrong
side

FLAT BAG

A bag that does not stand can be made of a single piece of fabric.

MATERIALS NEEDED
Fabric (or vinyl)
Yarn or cord (about 20")
Fabric glue
Edgings, trims (optional)
Also needed: Yarn needle, tape measure

CUT fabric to height of object plus 1¾". Lay piece around object to determine dimension needed. Add ½". Cut.

FOLD fabric in half, right sides together. Sew up ¼" side seam. Shift this seam to middle. Press seam open. Sew end closed (Fig. 1).

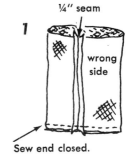

1

¼" seam

wrong side

Sew end closed.

TO FINISH TOP: The simplest way is to fold fabric over 1" and glue to inside of bag with fabric glue (especially practical for vinyl.) Turn bag right side out.

ATTACH cord in back. Fold yarn or cord in half. Sew at centerpoint in back about 1" below top of bag (Fig. 2). To close bag, gather around over object and tie bow in front.

2

Sew.

Back

Another method of closing a drawstring bag without a channel: Thread yarn on needle. Make a running stitch around top of bag, about 1" down. Stitches should be about ¾" long, starting at center front. Make last stitch about ¼" away from first (Fig. 3), pulling ends so equal lengths are out. Put object inside, pull on cord, and the top will be gathered closed. Tie a bow. This can be used on either a glued or sewed top.

TRIM: Now you can add decorations, if you like. Lay bag flat, use fabric glue to attach fringes, rickrack, edgings, etc. (Fig. 4). After top is tied, with gift inside, tie on package decorations or slip artificial flower into the top.

3

Front

4

rickrack

yarn fringe

VARIATIONS

Make bags in sets of three to sell at a bazaar, or for an unusual but practical gift. Suggested dimensions for cutting fabrics for these would be 6" (high) × 10" (around), 8" × 12", and 9" × 14".

FOOD PACKAGING

Any delicacy you make to give, or to sell at a bazaar, will be doubly appetizing if you wrap it attractively. Most gifts are wrapped to create an element of mystery and surprise, but the idea behind food packaging is to enhance the goodies and tempt the recipient. So use transparent containers for food gifts whenever possible. Add all the elegant, decorative trims you like, but make sure the treats are still visible.

Containers can be inexpensive and disposable. Or they can be durable enough to save after the food gift has been enjoyed. Suggestions are given here, but if you search about, and use your imagination, you are sure to find all sorts of novel ideas for attractive and reusable packaging.

GLASS JARS

Improvise as much as you wish in decorating glass jars but leave enough of the glass uncovered to show contents. An apothecary jar is good for this purpose and is a gift itself. When filled, seal top to jar with transparent tape so that contents do not spill.

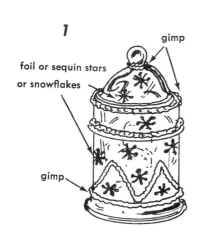

1

gimp

foil or sequin stars
or snowflakes

gimp

MATERIALS NEEDED
Apothecary jar
Gold gimp, foil motifs, colored soutache braid
Fabric glue
Transparent tape

GLUE trims around jar as shown or in any arrangement you like (Fig. 1).

VARIATIONS

Use two interestingly shaped glasses with identical-diameter rims. Fill each and gently set together, rim to rim. Tape together, glue trim over joining (Fig. 2). Add other trims as desired.

Use a single brandy snifter or footed goblet. Smooth plastic wrap over top and around sides. Tie and trim.

2

FOIL

Flat foil containers may either be new or washed-clean leftovers. Being disposable, they are an inexpensive way to present a food gift, and need little decorating.

MATERIALS NEEDED
Disposable foil pie plates, cake pans, etc.
Adhesive-backed vinyl (flower pattern)
Edging or trim
Cord

GLUE a trim around rim. For cake pans, cut out and stick on some flowers around side.

FILL and cover with clear plastic wrap. Tie with decorative cord or ribbon. Then stick on more cut-out flowers. Or tie on a couple of disposable picnic spoons or forks.

CANS

Round cans with lids make excellent containers, since these can be used later for canisters. They can be decorated in many ways.

MATERIALS NEEDED
Coffee container with plastic lid (or similar container)
Paint
Knob (or empty thread spool) with screw or bolt
Adhesive-backed burlap or vinyl (or other covering)
Cardboard (optional)
White glue
Epoxy putty (optional)

PAINT outside of can (or stick on or glue covering around can). Paint knob. Screw knob to lid. If there is a protruding portion of screw, cover end with epoxy putty. Allow to dry.

SIDES: Some coffee cans have ridges. If you wish to hide the coffee-can look, cut a piece of lightweight cardboard to exact size (so that edges do not overlap). Glue around can. This gives a smooth surface to decorate as you please.

EXAMPLES: Fig. 1 uses adhesive-backed burlap covering; Fig. 2, a modern effect of black and silver vinyl; Fig. 3 accentuates indentations by gluing decorations in the ridges.

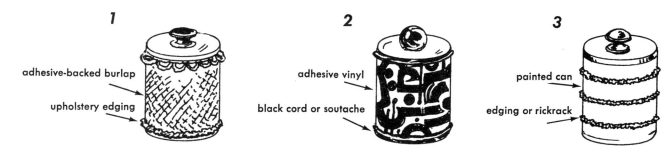

1 — adhesive-backed burlap / upholstery edging
2 — adhesive vinyl / black cord or soutache
3 — painted can / edging or rickrack

METAL CONTAINERS

These are useful for larger baked items.

MATERIALS NEEDED
Tin container with cover (from candies, cookies, fruitcake, etc.)
Paint
Suitable picture
Glitter
Blister (from small package, back removed)
Gift-wrap cord
White glue
Sequins

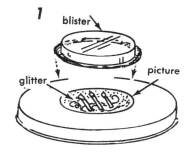

1 — blister / picture / glitter

CUT a greeting card or other picture in circular shape (or shape to suit top of can). Glue to top. Spread glue on parts of the picture and sprinkle with glitter. To keep neat, glue the round package blister over the card. The sparkle of the glitter is festive but it is a nuisance when it sheds, so use glitter only if it is possible to cover it (Fig. 1).

TO TRIM: Glue gift-wrap cord around picture over edge of blister. Glue on sequins or other trims.

VARIATIONS

Top may be trimmed with artificial-flower cluster (corsage or other orna-ment). With an awl, punch holes in top of lid. Attach flowers by wiring or tying on from the underside. Cut a circle of adhesive vinyl to fit cover and stick inside lid to hide wire ends.

Other elements that can be added: plastic or paper doilies (glue a picture in center), plastic wreath on round cans, artificial fruit, etc.

PLASTIC CONTAINERS

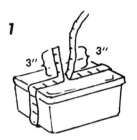

1

The scope of plastics available range from the most flimsy discardable type to solid dishes that can be reused for many purposes. Look about housewares departments and your own kitchen for ideas.

Refrigerator Dish

MATERIALS NEEDED
Rectangular plastic refrigerator container (covered)
Nylon net
Yarn or ribbon
Tape measure

2

TO DETERMINE SIZE TO CUT NET: Measure around the long dimen-sion of the dish. Add at least 3″ on each end of measure (Fig. 1). Cut a square of net this size.

SET REFRIGERATOR DISH (full of goodies) in the middle of the net square. Gather up net, and tie with yarn or ribbon (Fig. 2).

Tomato Basket

MATERIALS NEEDED
Plastic berry or tomato basket
Art foam, ⅛″ thick, or decorative ribbon
Spray paint (optional)
Yarn or cord
Plastic wrap
Fabric glue

SPRAY-PAINT plastic basket if desired.

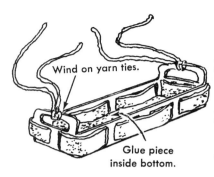

Wind on yarn ties.

Glue piece
inside bottom.

CUT strips of art foam the proper width to slide into basket. Or use proper width ribbon. Weave strips in and out. Glue ends if necessary.

WRAP cookies or candy; fill basket. Overwrap with clear plastic. Hold in place with yarn ties.

Berry Basket

MATERIALS NEEDED

Plastic berry basket

Cardboard (from cereal box or writing pad back)

Decorative paper

Adhesive-backed colored tape (fabric or plastic)

Foil

White glue

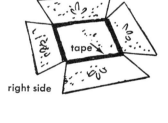

1

tape

right side

TO MAKE cardboard shape: Trace around one side and base of berry basket. Cut four side pieces and a base of the lightweight cardboard.

GLUE onto the five cardboard pieces any surfacing that is bright and colorful. (The one shown in the drawing was covered with red wallpaper from a sample book.) Attach the four sides to the base with tape (Fig. 1). Fold unit around basket, taping up corners.

LINE basket with foil. Fold foil outside, over top edge, and cut edges leaving about ¼" of foil over edge. Tape this foil to top edge (Fig. 2). Wrap food in clear wrap, tie at top, set in basket.

2   foil

Tape corners.

VARIATIONS

Basket can be used in its original form. Tie on tiny trinkets or ornaments, and glue ribbon or braid along top edge. Or weave yarn or paper strips through openings of the basket.

Round Plastic Containers

Small containers, packed in groups, make an unusual gift.

MATERIALS NEEDED

Three round plastic containers with plastic tops (from candied fruits,

whipped topping, etc.)
Colored plastic net, onion or potato bag
Decorative circular picture or motif (optional)
Yarn
Paper stars (from stationery store)

SLIDE the three filled containers into the bag. (You might like to stick a colorful design to top cover of top container before putting in bag.)

GATHER up top of bag over top of container. After tying bag closed, stick on stars back to back over net edges, as shown.

VARIATIONS
Plastic or copper pot scrubbers can be opened and used in a similar way to cover one or several small containers.

See color photograph facing page 153.

BASKETS

New or old baskets are ideal for gift wrapping. Handled baskets or round wicker trays can be used.

MATERIALS NEEDED
Basket; wicker, plastic (even an old Easter basket)
Gold spray paint
Decorative trims
Thin wire
Clear wrap
Ribbon or bow

SPRAY GOLD or a bright color, if basket is old. Allow to dry thoroughly.

TO DECORATE: Sew or wire trims onto basket. Place food in clear wrap, tie, set in basket. If basket is large, place food in clear containers, such as plastic glasses. Cover with clear wrap, tie gaily. Place several containers in the basket. Or line the basket with foil, add wrapped food, and cover entire basket with clear wrap. For color and variety, fruits or wrapped cheeses can be added with baked goods.

PAPER CONTAINERS

The least expensive packaging for food gifts are paper plates and disposable supermarket trays.

MATERIALS NEEDED
Disposable tray of papier-mâché or styrofoam
Gift-wrap
White glue
Clear wrap
Edging
Yarn ties or ribbon

COVER tray with gift-wrap paper (see page 159). Glue a trim around the edge.

WRAP food in clear wrap. Place food on tray. Wrap entire unit with clear wrap and tie with ribbon or yarn. Or hold together with colorful stick-on flowers.

VARIATIONS
Platters, dishes, and bowls in seasonal designs and colors, made of paper with a plastic finish, are sold in party and card shops. They make attractive gift packs and can be reused.

PACKAGING COOKIES FOR SHIPPING

Cookies may have to travel a great distance if they are sent to a loved one who has moved far away or to someone in the armed services. When shipping food gifts, it is wise to pack carefully and feel reasonably sure that they will arrive in good condition.

Containers may, of course, be decorated before packing for shipment. Here are some suggestions for packing.

MATERIALS NEEDED
Clear plastic wrap
Aluminum foil
Box or container
Tissue paper
Corrugated packing box
Masking or sealing tape
Brown wrapping paper
Sturdy cord
Transparent tape

WRAP COOKIES separately, or place two, back to back, in a clear plastic wrap. Tape or tie closed. Or use foil which will stay closed without fastening.

PACK in a container such as plastic shoe box, refrigerator dish, cardboard gift box, metal tin, coffee can with plastic lid, or any practical, unbreakable container. Fill container but don't crowd. Then add a padding of crushed tissue paper to prevent shaking.

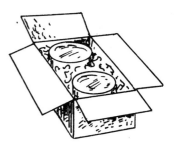

LINE A CORRUGATED packing box with aluminum foil. Crumple newspaper around sides or use shredded paper or foam (from notions department). Do not use edible packing, such as cereal or popcorn, since it can absorb fumes from engines and become unsafe to eat.

PLACE CONTAINER in corrugated box, packing tightly so it won't shift. Tuck in some plastic bags of individually wrapped hard candies, a homemade trinket, or other small surprises that may be welcome. Tape cover closed.

WRAP BOX tightly in heavy paper, seal with tape and tie with strong cord. Address the package in legible print. A covering of transparent tape over the address will help prevent water-marking or smearing.

Index